THE BEDFORD SERIES IN HISTORY AND CULTURE

Augustus and the Creation of the Roman Empire

A Brief History with Documents

Ronald Mellor

University of California, Los Angeles

BEDFORD/ST. MARTIN'S   Boston   ◆   New York

OUACHITA TECHNICAL COLLEGE

For Bedford/St. Martin's

Executive Editor for History: Mary V. Dougherty
Director of Development for History: Jane Knetzger
Developmental Editor: Elizabeth Morgan
Editorial Assistant: Shannon Hunt
Senior Production Supervisor: Joe Ford
Production Assistant: Matthew Hayes
Senior Marketing Manager: Jenna Bookin Barry
Project Management: Books By Design, Inc.
Indexer: Books By Design, Inc.
Text Design: Claire Seng-Niemoeller
Cover Design: Billy Boardman
Cover Art: Prima Porta Augustus. This idealized statue shows Augustus as a god after
  his death in 14 CE. On his ornate breastplate, mythological figures surround the
  emperor's stepson Tiberius receiving the lost Roman standards from the Parthian
  king in 20 BCE (see page 31). Vatican Museum, Rome. Photo from Art
  Resource, N.Y.
Composition: Stratford Publishing Services, Inc.
Printing and Binding: Haddon Craftsmen, an RR Donnelley & Sons Company

President: Joan E. Feinberg
Editorial Director: Denise B. Wydra
Director of Marketing: Karen Melton Soeltz
Director of Editing, Design, and Production: Marcia Cohen
Manager, Publishing Services: Emily Berleth

Library of Congress Control Number: 2005921357

For information, write: Bedford / St. Martin's, 75 Arlington Street, Boston, MA 02116
(617-399-4000)

ISBN: 0-312-40469-7 (paperback)
      1-4039-6805-5 (hardcover)
EAN: 978-0-312-40469-7

Acknowledgments

For Oliver Thorold and Genevra Richardson

Foreword

The Bedford Series in History and Culture is designed so that readers can study the past as historians do.

The historian's first task is finding the evidence. Documents, letters, memoirs, interviews, pictures, movies, novels, or poems can provide facts and clues. Then the historian questions and compares the sources. There is more to do than in a courtroom, for hearsay evidence is welcome, and the historian is usually looking for answers beyond act and motive. Different views of an event may be as important as a single verdict. How a story is told may yield as much information as what it says.

Along the way the historian seeks help from other historians and perhaps from specialists in other disciplines. Finally, it is time to write, to decide on an interpretation and how to arrange the evidence for readers.

Each book in this series contains an important historical document or group of documents, each document a witness from the past and open to interpretation in different ways. The documents are combined with some element of historical narrative—an introduction or a biographical essay, for example—that provides students with an analysis of the primary source material and important background information about the world in which it was produced.

Each book in the series focuses on a specific topic within a specific historical period. Each provides a basis for lively thought and discussion about several aspects of the topic and the historian's role. Each is short enough (and inexpensive enough) to be a reasonable one-week assignment in a college course. Whether as classroom or personal reading, each book in the series provides firsthand experience of the challenge—and fun—of discovering, recreating, and interpreting the past.

Lynn Hunt
David W. Blight
Natalie Zemon Davis
Ernest R. May

Preface

The empire created by Caesar Augustus remains the central historical fact shaping later European history. The languages and law of much of Europe derive from Rome, and European political ideas and religion recall the fact that for more than five centuries Rome implanted its roots throughout western Europe. Even the great fault-lines of modern Europe go back to Roman times: the Rhine river as the line between Germanic and Romance civilizations goes back to the first century CE, and the division between the Roman Catholic and Greek Orthodox churches stems from the emperor Diocletian's division of the empire in the late third century.

It was Augustus who, in his fifty-seven years in public life, created the Roman Empire. Though the Romans had conquered much of the Mediterranean before he became sole ruler in 30 BCE, their state was in mortal peril and their empire could well have broken apart. The Roman elite had never adapted the government of a small city-state to the rule of a multilingual collection of territories. Augustus reconstructed the Roman state and enabled it to survive in a recognizable, but profoundly different, form—as a genuine empire. The Roman Peace that he established allowed a Greco-Roman cultural synthesis to diffuse throughout the western Mediterranean; it also permitted the expansion of Christianity and, after the conversion of the emperor Constantine in 313 CE, Christianity's domination of the European continent as the official state religion. If modern European history begins with the Italian Renaissance, it was the legacy of Rome that inspired that powerful movement of "rebirth." The very name Caesar Augustus has echoed down through the centuries. His successors at Rome adopted his names (*Augustus; Caesar*) and titles; even the modern titles of tsar, emperor, and kaiser hark back to his illustrious reign. He has assuredly left his stamp on European history.

A NOTE ABOUT THE TEXT

The purpose of this book is to allow students to use primary sources to evaluate Augustus' achievements. If all historians acknowledge the seminal importance of Augustus and the Roman Empire, there is still much debate—as there was in his own time—about the motivations of the first emperor. The only surviving eyewitness account is the self-serving *Res Gestae* (*Achievements of Augustus*) that Augustus composed in his seventy-sixth year and had inscribed on bronze and stone throughout the empire. But that is hardly adequate. Since Augustus and his family ruled Rome for a century, few opponents could speak publicly against the Julio-Claudian family and dissenting views can usually only be found scattered in later writers. So we must look to a wide variety of sources—histories, poems, biographies, inscriptions, laws, and images—as well as the words of Augustus himself, in order to examine the emperor's accomplishments.

In this volume I have collected documents and images representing this range of sources. The images are not merely for illustration, but are themselves documents of the political ideology of the Augustan Age. I have also provided a comprehensive introduction to the political, military, social, and cultural history of Augustus' reign to enable students to place these disparate documents into a coherent context and to address issues such as the creation of the Empire, the reform of administration, the cultural context of political change, and the personality of the emperor himself. The glossary of Greek and Latin terms, map, genealogy, chronology, study questions, and selected bibliography will enable students to formulate their own reactions to the documents and draw their own conclusions about how well Augustus succeeded.

The Principal Literary Sources for the Age of Augustus provides brief descriptions of the most important sources. While I have myself translated some of the sources from Latin and Greek, I have in most cases adapted and modernized older translations to make them more easily readable while remaining faithful to the original. The dates given in the headnotes are the dates of the sources themselves, not of the events described in them.

ACKNOWLEDGMENTS

Many colleagues and students have helped me with this book from long before its formal inception until publication. My UCLA colleague Lynn Hunt commissioned it and provided guidance. Other UCLA friends read the early draft and made many detailed suggestions: Stephen Chappell, Robert Gurval, and Jason Moralee. I am especially grateful to the reviewers for Bedford/St. Martin's, who made substantial suggestions for improvement both to the initial proposal and to the draft manuscript: John Bodel, Brown University; Christopher Carlsmith, University of Massachusetts Lowell; Daniel Garrison, Northwestern University; Michael Maas, Rice University; Thomas R. Martin, College of the Holy Cross; Nathan Rosenstein, The Ohio State University; Richard Talbert, University of North Carolina; W. Jeffrey Tatum, Florida State University; and Lawrence Tritle, Loyola Marymount University. Some were critical of the individual texts selected (or omitted), but all of their comments were extremely helpful as I tried to reconsider how students might be able to use individual documents. Their comments on my introduction forced me to rethink and rephrase many aspects of it. I deeply appreciate the time and energy these scholars devoted to this small book. While I could not adopt every suggestion without making the book twice as long, I did think seriously about every one of them, and used them to make a better book.

At Bedford/St. Martin's I must thank Patricia Rossi, Mary Dougherty, and Jane Knetzger, history editors; Elizabeth Morgan, development editor; and Emily Berleth and Nancy Benjamin, project editors for this book. They have been supportive throughout the process.

For Oliver and Genevra Thorold, this *libellum* is a small acknowledgement of your warm friendship across the decades.

Ronald Mellor

Contents

The Documents   **57**

1. **The Rise of Octavian**   **59**

    1. Augustus, *The Achievements of Augustus,* 14 CE   59

    2. Nicolaus of Damascus, *On Julius Caesar's
        Admiration for the Young Octavius,* 20s BCE   69

    3. Suetonius, *On the Ides of March: The Assassination
        of Julius Caesar,* Second Century CE   70

    4. Appian, *On Octavian's First Confrontation
        with Antony,* Second Century CE   72

    5. Marcus Tullius Cicero, *Letters Revealing His Views
        of Young Octavian,* 44 BCE   74

    6. Appian, *On the Second Triumvirate,* Second
        Century CE   77

    7. Tacitus, *A Senatorial View of the Civil War,* Second
        Century CE   80

    8. Plutarch, *On Cleopatra's Seduction of Mark Antony,*
        Second Century CE   82

    9. Cassius Dio, *On Octavian's Propaganda against
        Antony,* Third Century CE   84

    10. Suetonius, *On Antony's Propaganda against Octavian
        in 34 BCE,* Second Century CE   85

    11. Cassius Dio, *On the Conquest of Egypt,* Third
        Century CE   86

2. **Augustus as** *Princeps*   **90**

    12. Suetonius, *On the Restoration of the Republic,* Second
        Century CE   90

    13. Cassius Dio, *On the Illness of Augustus in 23 BCE,*
        Third Century CE   91

    14. Suetonius, *Some Anecdotes and Descriptions
        concerning Augustus,* Second Century CE   92

    15. Macrobius, *On Augustus' Sense of Humor,* Fifth
        Century CE   94

Illustrations

PART ONE

Introduction: From Octavian to Augustus

On August 19, 14 CE, in the month bearing his own name, Caesar Augustus died in his seventy-sixth year. As the first Roman emperor, he had exercised nearly absolute power for an extraordinary forty-five years and his enduring legacy was the transformation of Rome and of the Mediterranean world. During the first century BCE, the Roman Republic was beset by civil war and domestic unrest. The senatorial class was trying to maintain the traditional form of government in the face of insubordinate armies, the urban masses, and a restive provincial population. Pompey and Julius Caesar, Cicero and Cato, Brutus and Marc Antony had fallen to their enemies in the civil wars between 49 and 30 BCE that ended with the triumph of Octavian, the heir of Julius Caesar. But that success could have been as temporary as the earlier triumphs of Pompey and Caesar. Why and how did this young man rise to power, and how did he manage to control the state for decades? How did he ensure social stability, restructure the Roman army, and begin two centuries of the Roman Peace (*Pax Romana*)? How, under the name of Augustus, did he inspire a cultural and religious revival? How did he create the ideology and institutions of a new political structure—the Roman Empire—which would survive in Rome for another five centuries? The documents in this volume will sketch important elements in a reign that has transformed the history of the West.

1

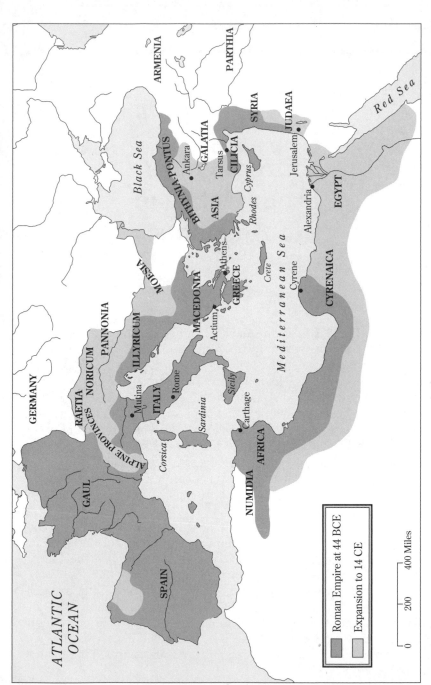

The Roman Empire in the Time of Augustus, 44 BCE–14 CE.

THE COLLAPSE OF THE ROMAN REPUBLIC

In the five hundred years since the Romans expelled the Etruscan kings in 509 BCE, the Roman Republic had expanded to include nearly the entire Mediterranean world (see map). The Romans viewed themselves as sturdy, honest farmers who were devoted to the gods, to the Republic, and to their families. But their remarkable success transformed these serious and conservative conquerors. Their small farming community gradually subjugated their neighbors in central Italy, then defeated the older civilizations of the Etruscans to the north and Greeks to the south. By the end of the third century BCE, Rome controlled all of Italy as well as the fertile island of Sicily. By the second century BCE, Rome had destroyed Carthage and defeated the Hellenistic kingdoms of the eastern Mediterranean. Rome had in the process made provinces of Spain, North Africa, Greece and Macedonia, western Asia Minor, and southern Gaul (now France).

The success of imperial expansion brought to Rome treasure, slaves, and art, as well as changing values and new cultural attitudes.[1] The vast wealth and power of the Empire sharpened social and economic conflict among the Roman people. In some areas, like southern Italy and Sicily, large senatorial estates were worked by captured slaves, while many Roman peasants sold their lands to move into the cities to find work.[2] Many Roman nobles, who had for centuries competed to show their devotion to the Republic, now placed wealth and personal comfort above patriotic duty. Some even began to emulate the luxurious and sophisticated life found in Greek cities, and they competed with each other in erecting elaborately painted villas, pursuing Greek culture, and amassing retinues of clients and slaves.

The historian Sallust believed that after the destruction of Carthage in 146 BCE, Rome had no external enemy, and so it slipped into corruption and internal civil discord. The jobless urban populace became angry and restless. Tiberius and Gaius Gracchus in turn were elected tribunes of the people (133–121 BCE) — an office designed to protect the interests of the Roman masses. They proposed a redistribution of public land and other popular reforms. The issues were complex, but the results were clear; both Tiberius and Gaius were murdered by senatorial gangs. Violence had been used to settle political conflict, and this set the pattern for the next century.

The concentration of land had another unfortunate effect. Because property was required for enlistment in the army, fewer Romans were eligible.[3] When German tribes defeated Roman troops in southern Gaul in 107 BCE and threatened to invade Italy, the general Marius recruited the landless poor with a promise to give them land upon their discharge. After his armies successfully defeated the Germans, Marius began a tradition of armies recruited by, and loyal to, their general. The terrible consequences became clear as armies followed their leaders—even against other Roman legions.[4]

Other dangerous trends developed as well. The inhabitants of Italy who were not Roman citizens had fought abroad as part of the Roman army, but they received few rewards. In 90 BCE, they rose in a terrible rebellion called the War of the Allies (or Social War) and gained citizenship, but they never truly gained political or social equality. They, and the provincials, chafed under the tax collectors and the arrogance of Roman officials. Meanwhile, as the rewards of political office grew, the competition for election became fiercer.[5] The combination of these elements produced a continuing civil unrest that threatened to destroy the unity of the state itself. Had the Romans conquered the Mediterranean merely to see themselves destroyed by their own success?

While individuals and groups struggled for power, few seemed willing to address the root causes of Rome's turmoil:

1. Rome administered a vast empire through institutions developed for a small city, and only a few dozen senators served as magistrates and administrators at any one time.
2. Much of the wealth of the state flowed into the hands of senators to finance their political struggles at Rome.
3. Unprecedented wealth of the elite and extreme poverty of the Roman masses threatened the unity of the state.
4. Without a regular budget or civil service, the state relied on private, and often corrupt, entrepreneurs to collect taxes, build roads, and provision the troops.
5. The **Italians*** remained excluded from full participation in the political, social, and economic life of Rome.
6. The soldiers gave their primary loyalty to the generals who recruited and rewarded them.

The Roman aristocracy did what they had done for centuries: they made speeches, they made deals, and they ran for office, because oratory, alliances (called *amicitiae*), and electoral success were the staples of Roman political life. Some knew, however, that the old structures were inadequate. Roman writers described this crisis, as they did all

---

*Boldfaced terms are defined in the glossary beginning on page 173.

crises, as the result of moral corruption. Whether the causes of decline were political, economic, or moral, the Republic was in serious danger. Contending generals set Rome's armies against each other, and the urban masses were easily aroused by politicians called *populares* for their aggressive support of the *populus Romanus* (the Roman people).

In 60 BCE, the three most powerful leaders formed a personal alliance, which historians call the First **Triumvirate**. (Their contemporary Varro called it a "three-headed monster.") Crassus needed to bail out his business allies who had overbid on government contracts, Pompey needed land for his troops, and Julius Caesar wished to administer a province. They controlled an unprecedented combination of wealth and political power. Caesar went to Gaul for ten years (58–49 BCE), where he gained immense booty from conquered peoples, built a reputation as a military genius, and won the loyalty of his troops. Crassus was less fortunate: in 53 BCE, he led an army against Parthia, where he lost three legions and his own life. Challenged by his senatorial opponents who enticed Pompey to their side to "save the Republic," Caesar illegally brought his armies from Gaul into Italy on January 10, 49 BCE, with the dramatic statement, "The die is cast." Over the next three years, this man of consummate political skill, military ability, and personal charisma defeated Pompey and the senatorial forces in Greece, Africa, and Spain. Many hoped his victory would at last bring peace, but others feared Caesar would become a king. In the five centuries since the Etruscans, Romans had held kings in contempt. Although Caesar had accepted the title of *dictator,* in February of 44 BCE, in a piece of political theater, he had scornfully turned down the royal crown. Nevertheless, he was a monarch in all but name.[6]

On March 15, 44 BCE, the Ides of March, a group of senators led by Marcus Junius Brutus assassinated Julius Caesar (see Document 3). Brutus' ancestor had led the rebellion against the last Tarquin king five centuries earlier, so he thought it his duty to strike down the "tyrant," even though Caesar had been his friend. The assassins shouted "Liberty! Freedom! Tyranny is dead!" and Brutus proudly issued coins bearing an image of daggers and the words, "The Ides of March." The conspirators expected that Caesar's death would restore the **Senate's** domination of the Roman government. This was an illusion. The ancient Republic was dead; Caesar's army was now the true source of Roman political power. Who would now control it? Who would hold together the Roman state?

At this point, the Romans had subjugated most of the Mediterranean basin (see map), but they had not yet imprinted their language, law, culture, and values on the conquered territories. In fact,
they had not yet learned to govern, as opposed merely to exploiting,
the provinces. If Roman politicians and generals had continued to turn
their armies against each other for the indefinite future, the state
would in time have fallen apart and the Greco-Roman synthesis would
never have come into being. For only under the Roman Empire
(27 BCE–476 CE), which brought with it the longest period of peace
and prosperity that the Mediterranean world had yet known, did
Rome became a world power. During that time Roman culture spread
throughout Europe so that Greek civilization and Christianity come to
us filtered through a Roman prism. For that to happen, the Roman
Peace still had to be secured, and the political and religious institutions, economy, administration, and army of the Roman Republic had
to be transformed into the Roman Empire.

THE RISE OF OCTAVIAN

The assassins were naïve. Caesar's troops were not appeased by a senatorial decree that freedom had been restored; they sought to guarantee the privileges Caesar had given them and to exact revenge for
their fallen general. The Roman masses were perhaps briefly aroused
by the ringing shouts of "Freedom!" and the celebratory bonfires, but
all that soon passed. Caesar's will, read in the Forum by his colleague
as **consul,** Marc Antony, gave 300 **sesterces**—four months' pay—to
every male Roman citizen, and bequeathed Caesar's extensive private
gardens to the Roman people. Stirred up by Antony's speech, crowds
of Romans furious over Caesar's death drove Brutus and his allies
from the city.

Antony had served under Caesar for ten years, and he was the *dictator*'s political deputy in Rome. He seemed to be Caesar's logical successor, and rumors had long circulated that he would be adopted by
Caesar. He quickly seized command of Caesar's troops and control of
his war chest, but there was another, unexpected claimant to Caesar's
wealth and, more important, to his name. In his will, Caesar had post-
humously adopted his eighteen-year-old great-nephew Gaius Octavius,
who was then studying and training across the Adriatic in Apollonia.
Almost at once, that inexperienced youth revealed the courage, intelligence, ruthlessness, and self-control that would later bring him mastery of the Roman world as the emperor Augustus (Figure 1).

Figure 1.
*Octavian
in 44 BCE.*
Bust of the young Octavian at age eighteen, wearing a beard as a sign of mourning after the assassination of Julius Caesar. *Musée de l'Arles antique, Arles, France.*
Erich Lessing/Art Resource, N.Y.

Who was Octavius? The Octavii were a wealthy but politically undistinguished family. At the time of Octavius' birth in 63 BCE, none of the Octavii had ever held high office, but his mother, Atia, was the daughter of Julia, the sister of the rising politician Julius Caesar. In 61 BCE, the boy's father died, and Caesar (now in Gaul) did what he could for his great-nephew. In 52 BCE, the eleven-year-old Octavius delivered the funeral oration for his grandmother Julia. After Caesar defeated Pompey in 48 BCE, young Octavius' career began with his assumption of the *toga virilis* (man's toga) and election to a priest-hood. Although illness prevented his participation in Caesar's African war against the republicans, Octavius rode behind Caesar in the **triumph** of 46 BCE. The following year, the young man went to Spain, where Caesar was fighting Sextus Pompey, the son of his old rival. At this point, Octavius became closer to Caesar, or so he later claimed. For example, we are told by later sources (which probably relied on Augustus' lost autobiography) that the *dictator* often asked the young man's advice (see Document 2). Caesar was a busy man in the last year of his life. He not only kept a traditional Roman household with his wife Calpurnia but also had a villa across the Tiber for the Egyptian queen Cleopatra and their baby son, Caesarion. He was preparing a large legislative program and planning a military campaign against Parthia. Nevertheless, it was at this time that he developed sufficient respect and affection for Octavius to write a secret will in which he not only gave his great-nephew three-quarters of his property but also adopted him as his son. (It was relatively common for a Roman nobleman without a son to adopt a young relative to keep his family name alive and ensure that his family cult would survive.) Late in 45 BCE, Caesar sent Octavius with his close friends Agrippa and Maecenas across the Adriatic, where the *dictator* had established headquarters for his anticipated Parthian campaign. Octavius was there when he heard of Caesar's murder a few days after the Ides of March.

Crossing to southern Italy against the advice of his mother and stepfather, Octavius learned of Caesar's will and took the name Gaius Julius Caesar Octavianus—following the custom of taking the adoptive father's name and keeping a form of his old family name as an added name. (He preferred to be called "Caesar," but writers from Shakespeare to the present call him "Octavian" to avoid confusion.) Antony had been spending Caesar's war treasury freely and he claimed to find justification for his actions in Caesar's papers, which he had impounded; his naked ambition alarmed the Senate and even offended many of Caesar's followers. By the late summer of 44 BCE, Octavian had begun to recruit Caesar's troops to defend his inheritance. He held no state office, while Antony was still consul, yet his name and loans from Caesar's wealthy friends allowed him to assemble a private army and pay the 300 sesterces that Caesar had bequeathed to each citizen (which Antony had refused to pay). Cicero and other senators flattered Octavian ("the divine youth") and furiously denounced what they saw as the real danger, Antony (see Document 5). After war broke out, Octavian and the consuls defeated Antony in northern Italy in April 43 BCE and caused him to withdraw to Gaul. When both consuls fell on the battlefield, Octavian expected to be rewarded, but the senators thought they could now ignore the nineteen-year-old youth. In the year after Caesar's murder, Octavian had learned well the arts of political psychology and dissemblance (see Document 4). Although he forced the Senate to name him consul in August 43 BCE, he understood that the senators would discard him as soon as they were free of Antony. Octavian paid an enormous bonus of almost ten years' salary to his troops to secure their loyalty, while he took diplomatic steps to make peace with Antony and reunite the Caesarian forces.

In November 43 BCE, Octavian, Antony, and Caesar's former aide, Marcus Lepidus, met near Bologna and formed a new triumvirate "for restoring the state." They gave themselves the authority to make law, to name consuls and other magistrates, and to command Rome's armies (see Document 6). As they marched toward Rome, they issued death warrants for their opponents. Even the great orator Cicero was struck down on a road near his villa. Many escaped to join Brutus and Cassius in the East, but their lands were confiscated and sold. The *triumvirs* used executions not only to purge their opponents but also to raise funds to pay their troops for the coming war.

The triumvirs could now turn their attention to avenging the murder of Julius Caesar, whom they consecrated as a god at the beginning of 42 BCE. The senatorial forces had control of the eastern Mediterranean for two years, imposing taxes on the provinces and confiscating money to pay their armies. Even the idealistic young poet Horace, later so close to Augustus, had left his studies in Athens to follow Brutus into battle to defend the Republic (see Document 45). In 42 BCE, Antony and Octavian took their army to northern Greece, and met Brutus and Cassius near the town of Philippi. They were the two largest Roman armies ever to confront each other. Antony's army fought well and, thinking Brutus had been defeated, Cassius committed suicide. Without his experienced ally's advice, Brutus did not take advantage of his ample supplies to outwait the enemy. Pressured by his troops to take action, he engaged in battle unnecessarily, and himself committed suicide after his defeat. It was not a great personal military success for Octavian (who was reportedly sick during the decisive battle), but Antony could now for the first time claim a major victory and stand as the military heir of the avenged Caesar.

The triumvirs embarked on a program of pacification of the East and resettlement of both the Caesarian and republican armies. Antony took on the more desirable task: the administrative reorganization of the wealthy eastern provinces. There, like earlier Roman governors, he gained personal wealth and the loyalty of both his troops and Rome's dependent monarchs. One of them was Cleopatra of Egypt, whom Antony had known during her years as Caesar's lover. Although Cleopatra may not have been considered a great beauty, she spoke nine languages and had personal charm and a remarkable intelligence (Figure 2b). Antony met her again at Tarsus in 41 BCE and took up with her where Caesar had left off (see Document 8).

(a) Denarius of Marc Antony and Octavian.

(b) Cleopatra.

(c) Augustus Conquers Egypt.

Figure 2. *Coins of the Age of Augustus.*

(a) Silver denarius issued by Antony and Octavian after their agreement at Brundisium in 40 BCE. Each triumvir appears on one side.

Photos by David Garstang.

(b) Bronze coin issued by Cleopatra VII, who was queen of Egypt for twenty-one years.

Courtesy of the Hunterian Museum, Glasgow.

(c) The legend "AEGYPT CAPTA" on this Roman coin of 28 BCE celebrates the conquest of Egypt; the crocodile made the event clear even to the illiterate. *British Museum, London.*

Photo by Werner Forman/Art Resource, N.Y.

Octavian's tasks were far less pleasant. He had to confront Sextus Pompey, whose fleet of republican exiles still controlled much of the western Mediterranean and could disrupt Rome's food supply. Even more challenging was Octavian's need to find land in Italy on which to settle the demobilized armies, lest they roam unrestrained across the Roman world. This task required confiscations and inevitably caused resentment and even rebellion. Antony's brother and wife, Fulvia, led angry landholders in a widespread rebellion against the expropriations, in what might have been a fatal blow against Octavian. The rebels were finally trapped in Perugia. Octavian pardoned the two leaders out of respect for his ally, then brutally slaughtered the fighters and city councilors of Perugia. (The story that he also sacrificed three hundred senators on the altar of the deified Julius seems to have come from Antony's later propaganda campaign, but the reality was savage enough.) Octavian here increased his reputation for ruthless cruelty, but ever the shrewd politician, he won the loyalty of his troops with land distribution. He now turned, like his father Julius Caesar, to building a political base among the leading citizens of the Italian towns.

Eventually ambition and mutual suspicion between the triumvirs almost led to war in 40 BCE, when Antony sailed to the Italian port of Brundisium, but the **centurions** of both armies—many of whom had fought together under Caesar—forced their leaders to compromise (see Figure 2a). Antony married Octavian's widowed sister, Octavia, and Octavian married Scribonia, a relative of Sextus Pompey. The triumvirs reached an agreement with Sextus at Misenum to lift his blockade of the shipments of grain. When Antony left Rome in October 39 BCE, he would never return. Although Octavia followed him to his headquarters in Athens, two years later Antony resumed his love affair with Cleopatra and publicly acknowledged his children by her.

In 37 BCE, the triumvirate was renewed for another five years. In 36 BCE, through the brilliance of his friend and admiral, Agrippa, Octavian defeated the impressive fleet of Sextus Pompey, whom his propaganda later dismissed as a "pirate." Finally, Lepidus, the weakest of the triumvirs, attempted to seize Sicily, but Octavian easily won over the loyalty of his troops and took his provinces. Because Lepidus had been *pontifex maximus* (high priest) since the death of Caesar, Octavian respectfully allowed him to live under house arrest in a country villa until his death twenty-four years later.

In the East, Antony's destiny became increasingly enmeshed with that of Cleopatra. By 36 BCE, she had borne him three children, and he had even gone through an Egyptian marriage ceremony. Why did

Antony do so? Antony may have entered into this marriage because in the multicultural world of Alexandria these celebrations provoked enthusiasm, and Antony needed Egyptian resources for his coming expedition against Parthia. But Antony's Parthian campaign was a humiliating calamity. He lost much of his army, although he heroically led the survivors back to safety. Had he defeated Parthia, his repute as a military leader would have been indisputable. Two years later, he tried to retrieve his reputation by launching a war against a much weaker Armenia. He celebrated that victory with an extravagant triumph in Alexandria, at which he bestowed Rome's eastern provinces on his children by Cleopatra. This act was portrayed in Rome as part of his unmanly submission to the queen: to hold a triumph away from Rome was considered a sacrilege to Jupiter! The eastern panoply played into Octavian's hands, as did Antony's repudiation and divorce of Octavia in 32 BCE.

The 30s BCE was a decade of vicious propaganda, which infects all the sources (see Documents 9 and 10). Although Suetonius' biography of Augustus survives, no complete narrative of the reign exists. Appian's *Civil Wars* gives a good account as far as 35 BCE, when it breaks off. Cassius Dio's narrative is comprehensive until 6 BCE, but the last twenty years (6 BCE–14 CE) contain many gaps. These later writers all depend on sources that survived until their time, but the descendants of Augustus and his wife Livia (whom he married in 38 BCE) held power for a century, so the sources were obviously heavily biased toward Augustus. Octavian played on Roman prejudice against easterners to pillory Antony: that he planned to make Cleopatra queen of Rome; that he would move the capital itself to Alexandria; and that his will said he wished to be buried in Alexandria. Octavian depicted himself as a Roman traditionalist. Antony might appeal to surviving republicans who were repelled by the cruelty and naked dynastic position of Caesar's heir, but Octavian focused his propaganda and his resources at the armies, the urban masses, and the Italian elite. He extended his patronage throughout Italy, and incorporated many Italians into his regime. He launched military campaigns in Illyricum between 35 and 33 BCE both to give himself an aura of military success and to train his armies for the inevitable war. His coins depicted himself with Venus, and his building program in Rome emphasized his links with the past. The balance of prestige had begun to tilt toward Octavian, who boldly compared his military success in Illyricum— modern Croatia—with Antony's Parthian disaster.

By 32 BCE, the triumvirate had ended. Because both consuls were sympathetic to Antony, Octavian's legal position was shaky. They feared his ambition and fled to Antony with, we are told, several hundred senators. In 31 BCE, Octavian declared war on Cleopatra, as though she alone was Rome's enemy, and sailed with his flotilla to Greece. Yet many of those senators and republican sympathizers, quickly disenchanted when they witnessed Antony's own ambitions and his subservience to Cleopatra, soon fled back to Octavian. They had trouble deciding which alternative was worse. Antony's delays allowed Agrippa to position Octavian's armies favorably. Having suffered numerous defections, Antony was outnumbered and defeated at the sea battle at Actium. He and Cleopatra fled to Egypt, abandoning much of their army and fleet to Octavian.

Octavian returned to Italy to settle his and Antony's troops, because the lovers were now powerless to stop his advance into Egypt. Following a battle near Alexandria a year later, Antony committed suicide. After an unsuccessful attempt to entice Octavian to become her third Roman lover, Cleopatra chose suicide rather than be led as a prisoner in Octavian's Roman triumph (see Documents 11 and 46). Although the victor spared Cleopatra's children by Antony, his men hunted down and murdered Caesarion, Caesar's son. The boy was a potential rival to Caesar's adopted son, and only one "Caesar" could be left alive. Because victors win the privilege of writing history, the writers of the Augustan Age so entangled Antony's memory in political propaganda and historical romance that the myths will forever obscure the historical reality of a fine general, an ambitious politician, and a generous extrovert, who has been branded "the triple pillar of the world transform'd into a strumpet's fool" (Shakespeare, *Antony and Cleopatra,* 1.1.13–14).

If we can never fully understand the motivations of Antony, we can appreciate why Octavian needed not only to defeat Antony but to bring Egypt under complete Roman control for the first time (see Figure 2c). Any new constitutional order would be worthless without his pacifying the mob and bringing the soldiers under control—and that would take a great deal of money. The greatest single source of wealth in the Mediterranean was the extraordinary fertility of the Nile valley—the huge barges that for millennia had brought surplus grain to the Delta, whence it could be traded throughout the Near East for cedar and luxury goods (see Document 11).

The products of Egypt—glass, ivory, and papyrus—were welcome in Rome, but its agricultural fertility was what made Egypt unique. Octavian saw the opportunity to stabilize the capital's grain supply and ameliorate the social tensions that had ravaged Rome since the Gracchi (see Figure 3). How much grain? One-third to one-half of Rome's grain came from Egypt: as much as 100,000 tons a year.[7] Although most of the capital's grain still came from North Africa and Sicily, Egyptian imports would not only stabilize the city's food supply but also provide adequate grain for the army. The surplus would eliminate the food confiscations that aroused so much anger among provincials. To gain permanent and secure access to this food supply, Octavian had to replace the last Ptolemy (Cleopatra) with some form of Roman administration. Within weeks after the death of Cleopatra, Octavian proclaimed himself Pharaoh. He kept Egypt as his personal possession—it never became a normal province—and he and his successors ruled it through a **prefect of Egypt** from the equestrian order; senators were even banned from visiting Egypt. The emperor understood the value of Egypt, and its danger in the hands of a rival.

The Republic had had no standing army. For a century, the great generals had recruited their soldiers and rewarded them either with booty from conquest or with land gained through their political position to support the soldiers and their families. For the last twenty years, however, these armies had been fighting each other—not much booty there! When Octavian had tried to find land to settle the veterans of Philippi, he inflamed civil war in Italy. Now he again needed to retire an enormous number of troops—his own and those of Antony—and establish a permanent army with a central treasury, if he were to have any hope of ending the cycle of armies following whichever general promised them the most. He also needed to embark on campaigns—in the Alps, in Spain, and along the Danube—to secure areas that had become unstable during the civil wars.

After the defeat of Cleopatra, Octavian was able to redeem his promises by using the accumulated treasure of the Pharaohs. His boast in his *Res Gestae* (*Achievements of Augustus*) that he actually *purchased* land for his troops after Actium was true, but the purchase occurred a year later, after Cleopatra's treasury was taken. So Egypt's treasure allowed Octavian to settle his troops and create a loyal standing army. When Augustus said at the end of his life that he had paid 2.5 billion sesterces of public expenses out of "his own money," we should remember that much of that money came from Egypt, which remained the personal property of the emperor (see Document 1).

Although there were occasional temporary food shortages, Egyptian wheat, along with that of north Africa, satisfied Rome's needs through the third century CE—an extraordinary feat in the fragile

Figure 3. *Bust of Octavian from Meroë.*
This bronze bust of Augustus was found beyond the Egyptian frontier at the
city of Meroë in Nubia. It seems to have been cut from a full-size statue set up
in Egypt soon after Cleopatra's death and then taken south as booty by a raid-
ing party during the 20s BCE. *British Museum, London.*
HIP/Scala/Art Resource, N.Y.

agricultural economy of the ancient world. Compared to the late
Republic, there was little civic unrest. After 330 CE, Egyptian wheat
was diverted to the new capital of Constantinople. Octavian had the
foresight to know that the grain and treasury of Egypt would provide
the economic means to reconstitute the Roman state in a new, more
stable, form. Without them, any new "constitutional" arrangement
would have been temporary.

Octavian was now the unchallenged master of Rome and her armies, and thus of the entire Mediterranean. Yet the defeat of Antony could no more resolve the conflicts consuming the Roman Republic than had Caesar's victory over his rivals. Octavian was only thirty-three, the same age as Alexander the Great when he died, but he would have another forty-three years of rule to address Rome's problems: demobilizing the huge armies and safeguarding their future loyalty; ensuring the safety of Rome's European frontiers, neglected during long civil wars in the East; reducing class hostility and civil unrest in the capital; making the Italians an integral part of Roman social, cultural, and political life; establishing an administrative apparatus to govern the Empire; and devising a form of monarchy that would avoid any resemblance to ancient Etruscan tyranny or to the eastern kingship, which had damaged the reputation of Antony.

After a year spent settling Antony's former territories in the East, the new leader returned to Rome in 29 BCE to celebrate his triumph (Figure 4). It was actually a triple triumph for victories in Illyricum, at Actium, and in Egypt. There was a great public spectacle, with an effigy of Cleopatra that was carried through the streets in the ceremonial procession to the **Capitoline Hill**, the political and religious focus of Rome. Octavian gave 400 sesterces apiece to a quarter million Roman **plebeians** (or **plebs**). The celebrations even included the closing of the gates of the Temple of Janus, which were only closed when the Romans were completely at peace. They had not been closed for more than two hundred years.

AUGUSTUS AS *PRINCEPS*

Now Octavian turned from winning the war to securing the peace, a task that most wise leaders have understood is far more difficult. In 28 BCE, Octavian again served as consul along with his loyal general Agrippa; the emergency was over and a general amnesty had been proclaimed. The same year saw the first celebration in Rome of the Actian Games. More than half of the sixty **legions** were being demobilized, and over 100,000 veterans pensioned off with grants of land. Wary of the insurrection that had followed his earlier land confiscations in 40 BCE, Augustus used the spoils of his successful Egyptian campaign to purchase land for some soldiers. Many were settled in new colonies founded in Italy and throughout the provinces.

The first step in Rome itself was to repair the bitter wounds of civil

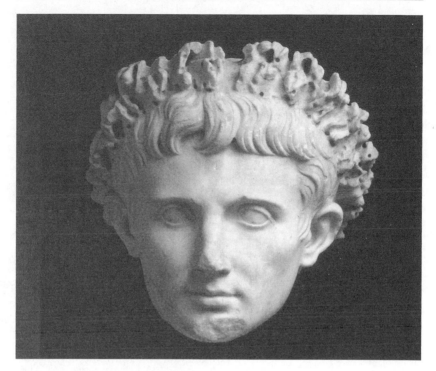

Figure 4. *Augustus with Crown.*
The emperor is depicted with the crown of a triumphant general—probably after his triple triumph of 29 BCE. Dressed like Jupiter and wearing a crown of laurel, the conquering general rode through Rome in a chariot before mounting the Capitoline Hill to pay tribute at the temple of Jupiter.
Réunion des Musées Nationaux/Art Resource, N.Y.

war. While he led his armies, the young Octavian had welcomed the title of *dux,* a title used informally for generals or party leaders during the civil wars. (Nineteen centuries later, Mussolini resurrected *dux* in his own title, *Duce.* His devotion to Augustus resulted in excavations of the Forum of Augustus and a massive celebration of the bimillennium of the birth of Augustus in 1937.) After 29 BCE, however, Octavian preferred to deemphasize those struggles. He was given the title of ***Princeps*** *senatus* (leader of the Senate), despite the fact that it had in the past usually been reserved for the most senior senator. The ruler and his advisors were giving serious thought to the names and titles that would define his place in the new regime.

On January 13, 27 BCE, in his own words, Octavian "transferred the Republic from my own power to the authority of the Senate and the Roman people." This was a carefully scripted piece of political theater: the Senate awarded him the additional name of *Augustus,* and mobs demanded that he retain power (see Document 12). Indeed, the people of Rome welcomed the end of civil war, the abundance of imported food, and the periodic distributions of money. They would continue to push enthusiastically for greater honors for Augustus, who presented himself as a *popularis* like Julius Caesar. The Senate was more grudging. Although many aristocrats may have lamented the demise of the Republic, others saw the real value of the Republic to be the protection of property and the security of life. New coins of 28 BCE had even proclaimed Augustus as the restorer of *libertas,* by which he meant that Romans were now free from the arbitrary use of force. Augustus' argument was that, by ending the civil wars, he had restored the Republic.

Octavian had initially thought of taking the name of the founder of Rome, Romulus, until second thoughts brought the realization that "Romulus" also carried unpleasant associations: he had been a king, and he had killed his brother Remus. So Octavian chose *Augustus,* which is related to the Latin words for growth (*augeo*) and authority (*auctoritas*), and carries positive connotations of both political authority and religious veneration. Octavian always preferred to attribute his dominance to *auctoritas* rather than the naked force implied in *potestas* (power). The sixth month in the Roman calendar, *Sextilis,* was renamed *Augustus,* as the fifth month had previously been named *Julius* after Julius Caesar.

This was the beginning of the astonishing transformation of the pitiless and ambitious young Octavian into the genial, cultured, and beloved Augustus (see Document 14). The senators set up an honorific gold shield to honor him in the Senate-house, and placed an oak crown of victory on the door of his home. In the legal fiction of restoring the Republic, Augustus modestly claimed that he held "no more power than the others who were my colleagues in each magistracy" (see Document 1). But Augustus did not derive power from his offices; his goal was to legalize, and veil, his real power, which came always from the army's loyalty and the elimination of rivals. A century after Augustus' death, the historian Tacitus wrote: He took on "himself the functions of the Senate, the magistrates, and the laws" (see Document 7).

Although Augustus held the consulship every year from 31 to 23 BCE, his power did not come from any single magistracy but from the authority of victory and a patchwork of powers carefully designed to avoid the hatred Caesar aroused with his dictatorship. The details were traditional; the totality, unprecedented. Again and again, he cloaked his political and ideological innovations under a guise of traditional Roman values. Since the 30s BCE, Octavian had used *imperator*—a title awarded to victorious generals—as part of his nomenclature; it comes down to us in English as "emperor." Senators preferred his adopted name of "Caesar," which eventually became a title of his successors. But, in 27 BCE, the Senate named Augustus *princeps* (leading man of the state), which later became the official title of the Roman emperors. Although we refer to the Roman Empire, the Romans called it a "principate," because it was ruled by a *princeps*. Augustus went to great lengths to avoid the titles of *rex* (king) and *dictator*. Fear of the first and the reality of the second had aroused a conspiracy against Julius Caesar; his heir would tread more carefully.

THE NEW CONSTITUTION

The third-century historian Cassius Dio created an imaginary debate between Augustus' closest advisors, Maecenas and Agrippa, on how the emperor should organize the new state (see Document 16). Of course neither Dio nor modern historians have had access to such discussions, but they must have occurred. The old system of government had obviously failed to adapt; in the first century BCE, Roman leaders had pursued their private ambitions to the detriment of the common good. Despite Cicero's and Brutus' rhetoric of liberty, only a few dozen men had controlled the fate of the Republic, and they had repeatedly brought it to civil war. Augustus felt he could do better, but how could he govern the state more effectively? The acquisition of power was not enough; Augustus had to guard against Caesar's fate as well as exercise power effectively. Could he restore Rome to order, or would the state once again slip into anarchy?

Scholars have described the new "constitution" of the Roman Empire. Of course there was no written constitution any more than there had been one for the Roman Republic. Rome's constitution had long been flexible; what was outrageous at one point, like immediately repeated consulships or tribunates, was acceptable later. So much that was unprecedented had happened during the civil wars that it is difficult for us—and perhaps was for the Romans—to grasp what was "normal" by 27 BCE. In the nineteenth century, scholars were interested in the legal and constitutional underpinnings of states. Thus Theodor Mommsen, who won the second Nobel Prize in Literature in 1902 for his *History of Rome,* thought that Augustus had established a dyarchy in which constitutional power was shared between the emperor and the Senate (see Document 34).[8] In the twentieth century, scholars have realized that—in the words of Mao Tse-tung—"political power comes from the barrel of a gun." Men like Hitler and Mussolini, Stalin and Mao, Kim Il Sung and Saddam Hussein cared little for legal niceties—they created constitutions suitable to their needs. So some historians in the twentieth century, like Sir Ronald Syme, saw Augustus' constitution as "a fraud and a façade."[9] But it was more than that. Augustus devoted so much time and effort to his "arrangements" that we must take them seriously (see Document 16).

We must remember that Octavian was not omniscient. He could not know that he would reign for forty-five years, nor exactly how the army, people, and senators would respond to his changes. Nor could he have hoped for the overwhelming popularity he later achieved with the Roman people. The transformation of Rome was so vast that later historians—even Romans like Tacitus and Cassius Dio—were tempted to see it as part of an overarching plan. Augustus began with less ambitious goals and had the political genius to adapt flexibly and pragmatically to changing circumstances. His motto was said to be *festina lente* (make haste slowly), and so his creation of the Empire's "constitution" was a gradual, adaptive process.

Multiple sources of political power existed in the Republic. A Roman consul—and there were always two—held **imperium** (military power), which carried the right not only to command an army but to exercise authority in Rome and to summon the Senate into session. Former consuls, called **proconsuls**, served as provincial governors (as Caesar did in Gaul) and held *imperium* over a specific territory. In 27 BCE, after Augustus' "resignation" of all special powers except his consulship, the Senate gave him, for ten years, proconsular *imperium* over the provinces of Syria, Spain, and Gaul, including the Rhine frontier. (Julius Caesar had held his proconsulship in Gaul for ten years.) Those provinces contained the great bulk of the Roman army— twenty of a total of twenty-eight legions. Because Augustus administered them through his deputies, called **legates**, he held effective control over the military apparatus of the Empire (see Document 35). The combination of powers was extraordinary but not unprecedented: in 52 BCE, Pompey had been consul in Rome and proconsul of Spain. As always, it was important to Augustus to link his powers to earlier precedents to emphasize the return of the Republic.

On his return from campaigning in Spain in 24 BCE, Augustus found discontent in the capital. Although the army and masses supported him, the senatorial oligarchy was grudging. There was a growing gap between the Senate's public fawning and private dissent. Early in 23 BCE, the *princeps* became very ill, so ill that he expected to die and gave his papers and signet ring to Agrippa, the only man who could have kept the armies united. When he recovered after several months, Augustus decided to change the structure of his rule. He recognized that he had been monopolizing the consulship, which he had held for nine consecutive years between 31 and 23 BCE. The consulship was the peak of ambition for Roman nobles, for through it they could equal the high achievements of their ancestors. Augustus needed the administrative expertise and institutional memory of these senators, yet he was blocking their career path. So in July 23 BCE, he resigned the consulship, and held it only two more times in the next thirty-seven years. It was a brilliant stroke: he relinquished the office while retaining the power in other ways.

The emperor retained his proconsular *imperium,* and now took a newly devised **tribunician power**, adapted from the powers the tribunes held during the Republic. This allowed Augustus wide powers, including the right to propose or veto legislation. He and his successors regarded it as so emblematic of imperial power that they dated their reigns on coins and inscriptions by the year of their tribunician power. The Senate also voted *imperium maius* (superior power to command), which gave Augustus primacy over all other consuls and proconsuls. He did not need to hold the consulship; he had all the effective powers of any consul.

It was probably in 22 BCE that a conspiracy was discovered; one consul and another senator were executed. This was one of several "conspiracies" that are poorly documented in the ancient sources. Over the five decades Augustus held power, we find occasional mention of executions, exiles, and suicides of the regime's opponents. Tacitus later called it "a peace stained with blood" (see Document 55). Details are usually murky, though, so it is unclear whether the opposition was ideological or personal. In any event, there seems to have been no widely organized opposition. Augustus was certainly confident enough to allow some writers to take jabs at him. Cremutius Cordus wrote a republican version of history in which he called Brutus "the last of the Romans." Cordus lived with impunity under Augustus, although he was prosecuted later under Augustus' paranoid successor, Tiberius.

There were repeated calls for Augustus to take even more power. A food shortage in 22 BCE led to riots, with the crowds demanding that Augustus become *dictator.* He took direct control of the grain supply, and the shortage soon disappeared. On other occasions, when he left Rome for extended stays in Asia (22–19 BCE) or Gaul (16–13 BCE), Rome saw unrest that only his reappearance calmed. We might suspect that the *princeps* was not unhappy to see popular passions unleashed in his favor; they allowed him to neutralize potential opposition from the senators.

Other titles and honors were heaped upon Augustus: consular *imperium* for life; **censor**, which enabled him to revise the roll of the Senate; *pontifex maximus,* the high priesthood once held by Julius Caesar; and finally, in 2 BCE, *pater patriae*—"Father of the Country." These offices and titles gave Augustus no real added power, for he already controlled every aspect of religious, civil, and military life. In fact, he held as much power as any absolute despot, but he knew enough to disguise it in republican trappings, to allow the senators to keep their pride and he their loyalty. We might regard these constitutional changes as a process of "negotiation" through which Augustus and the senators could reach a viable political consensus. Only later in the Empire did the law codes contain the famous clause: "What pleases the emperor has the force of law." Augustus held such power *de facto;* much later his successors would hold it *de jure.*

CREATING A NEW ELITE:
SENATORS AND EQUESTRIANS

Although Augustan propaganda emphasized the restoration of the Republic, the late Republic was a failed political system. Huge resources were expended every year in political campaigns, and the elected officials then turned their attention to recouping their fortunes in the provinces. The Republic never governed the provinces effectively; there was no civil service, and governors, like the magistrates in Rome, normally changed every year. In Augustan Rome, provincial funds had to go to the central government rather than to individuals for two reasons: (1) to fund the state and its army and (2) to prevent individuals from amassing the resources to challenge the emperor. Augustus had to create new administrative structures and, perhaps more important, to choose the men to staff his administration. The new role of the Senate was administrative, not legislative; rather than make policy, the senators gave advice and carried out the emperor's will. As governors, they lost many of their opportunities to amass personal fortunes. Augustus was less interested in the Senate than in individual senators, whom he used as policy advisors, provincial governors, military commanders, and senior administrators. He allowed them to maintain their honors and status, because he needed their expertise to manage his empire. There was to be a division of labor, if not of political power.

However, the Senate had been transformed by two decades of civil war; many of the gifted had been killed, and the various factions had made their own loyalists senators. Augustus was determined to reinvigorate the senatorial order, to eliminate the disloyal and incompetent, and to add his own new men. During the 30s BCE, Augustus had begun to surround himself with a group of loyalists, but he was shrewd and understood that not all the ambitious men he needed to gain power—the thugs of revolution—would be suitable for the administration of the Empire. Now he would need the nonpolitical class—men, often from Italy, who did not have the money, ancestry, or connections to get elected, but who had the energy and skill to administer. So Augustus "nominated" them to the assembly for election, and thus transformed the Senate.

Three times Augustus was given the authority of a censor to revise the membership roll of the Senate (see Document 18). The major changes of 28, 18, and 11 BCE were crucial to the success of the new regime. The first two reduced the Senate from 1,000 members to the 600 it had had in more normal times. Like any politician, the *princeps* turned first to supporters whose loyalty had been proven. During the civil wars, the Italians had been his most devoted followers and they were generously included in the new regime. Augustus even brought talented Italians into the Senate and high office by giving them sufficient funds to meet the minimum property qualification for all senators, one million sesterces—a thousand times a soldier's annual salary (see Document 19).

The emperor's vast wealth was central to his transformation of the Senate. He could bestow on the favored money, office, and honor—the most important elements for a Roman noble. Augustus took care not to humiliate the senatorial order; he built no large palace and avoided haughtiness and pomposity in his contacts with other Romans. He met frequently with a personal advisory council to keep in touch with a wide circle of senators. The Senate now acted as a court for charges brought against senators. Undoubtedly, many secret meetings were held in which Augustus solicited recommendations and identified talented young men for promotion or perhaps old adversaries for execution.

An empire of sixty million needed more administrators than the Senate could provide. Augustus turned to the equestrian order—those citizens possessing more than 400,000 sesterces—for a wide range of administrative tasks (see Document 20). The *equites* served in financial posts in Rome and abroad, where they even acted as governors in some smaller provinces such as Judaea, where the equestrian Pontius Pilate ruled in the 20s CE. As with the Senate, Augustus was prepared to provide the necessary funds to bring talented men into the equestrian order. The highest equestrian offices were posts with so much control over troops or the food supply that Augustus preferred not to entrust them to ambitious senators. The emperor remembered well republican generals like Pompey and Caesar, who had used their armies to seize power. Thus, on the model of the prefect of Egypt, the emperor gradually assigned new tasks to equestrian administrators called *prefects:* in 2 BCE, the two **prefects of the praetorian guard,** who controlled troops stationed in Rome and Italy; in 6 CE, the **prefect of the grain supply;** and, in 8 CE, the **prefect of the watch.** Even equestrians could have dangerous ambitions, though. The first prefect of Egypt, Cornelius Gallus, took credit for an unauthorized war, fell out of imperial favor, and committed suicide.

For the first time, Rome had the beginnings of a civil service, one that would be expanded and regularized under later emperors. The numbers were still small but larger than under the Republic, and competent officials held their posts for longer terms than earlier. A clear promotion ladder developed for senators and equestrians: for senators, the proconsulship of Asia was at the top; for equestrians, it was the prefectureships of Egypt and the praetorian guard. In time, retired centurions, often Italians or even provincials, were promoted to equestrian posts in the civil administration, while effective equestrians were promoted into the senatorial order. Augustus began a process that gradually brought far more social mobility into the Empire than the Republic had ever seen.

The new structure allowed Augustus to transfer many bureaucratic functions from private, profit-making companies to imperial employees. One of the notably corrupt aspects of republican administration was tax-collecting, in which companies overcharged provincials, speculated in grain, and frequently bribed Roman governors. Now taxes, whether collected by local cities, private employees, or civil servants, were supervised by imperial financial officials—not the local governor. Income flowed directly into the imperial treasury, and the provincials were treated far better than during the Republic (see Document 32).[10]

SOCIAL AND RELIGIOUS REFORM

Cicero approvingly quotes an older poet: "The Roman state rests on ancient customs and men of the old type." This appeal to traditional Roman values formed an essential part of Augustus' program to turn back the clock to an idealized Roman past before the calamity of civil war. He was shrewd enough to draw on the Romans' desire to attribute political conflict to moral decline. He proclaimed himself to be a moral reformer who would remedy the corruption of the political elite in the late Republic.

For the Romans, religion focused on relations between humans—individually or, more usually, collectively—and the gods who protected their city and their families. Religion reflected society, since gods and humans were members of a single community. If their community was troubled (as in civil war), Romans would attribute the difficulties to their neglect of the gods. The purpose of religion was to bring order and comprehensibility to a potentially chaotic world. Roman morality had less to do with the gods than with the Romans' own practices in following the *mores maiorum* (customs of the ancestors), the source of our own word "morality."

Augustus passed more legislation than any Roman leader before him, much of it directed at what he regarded as moral issues. Of course we recognize that legislation on marriage, inheritance, and the emancipation of slaves all was aimed at an increasing control of society. Because freed slaves automatically became Roman citizens, Augustan legislation tried to moderate this dilution of the citizen body (see Documents 28 and 29). His marriage reforms of 18 BCE and 9 CE may have been welcome to the lower classes, the army, and the Italian elite, who looked scornfully at changing sexual mores among the senatorial class. One senator, who praised the virtues of his dead wife, makes it clear that she was exceptional (see Document 27). Sexual promiscuity and the pursuit of political advantage had led to an increase in bachelorhood, divorce, and irregular liaisons among the upper classes. These changes had resulted in a marked decline in the aristocratic population already decimated by the civil wars. As a result, Augustus' program had not just a moral dimension but a practical one as well. Because the emperor needed Roman citizens to administer the Empire and serve in its legions, he passed legislation to encourage marriage and childbearing (Documents 25 and 26). The unmarried and the childless suffered political and financial penalties, while those with three or more children received special privileges. New inheritance laws aimed to keep property within the family and thus also strengthen marriage. Augustus made adultery a criminal offense, sending his own daughter and granddaughter into exile.

In addition to his moral legislation, Augustus revitalized many aspects of traditional Roman religion. He boasted that he revived old ceremonies, appointed the first *flamen Dialis* (priest of Jupiter) in many years, and restored eighty-two temples that had fallen into ruin (see Documents 1 and 23). In fact, the Romans of the late Republic were not so much neglecting these temples as turning attention to new forms of worship and building other temples. However, Augustus trumpeted his achievements as examples of his piety and traditionalism. He also built a dozen new temples, including one to Apollo, his patron at Actium, on the Palatine, and the splendid complex to Mars the Avenger in the Forum of Augustus to commemorate his victory over Caesar's murderers at Philippi. In 17 BCE, Augustus held splendid celebrations called "Secular Games" to mark the sacred anniversary of the founding of Rome and the arrival of a new Golden Age. In 13 BCE, he vowed to build the magnificent Altar of Augustan Peace (*Ara Pacis Augustae*), which was dedicated four years later. In 12 BCE, at the death of Lepidus, the emperor finally was elected *pontifex maximus* (Figure 5).

Despite Augustus' identification with Roman religious traditions, he also made innovations, like his deification of Julius Caesar through a temple built in his honor in the Forum. After Actium, Octavian was offered divine honors by cities he visited in the Greek East. This was no innovation; for two centuries, Greek cities had deified Roman generals, as they had earlier deified local kings. When the province of Asia set up such a cult, Octavian allowed himself to be worshipped only with the goddess Roma (Figure 6) and only by non-Romans (see Document 21). Worship of the emperor took many forms in the cities and provinces of the empire—from altars, games, and priesthoods, to the temples set up by the Gallic provinces at Lyons and by the Athenians on the Acropolis. This proliferation of emperor-worship was not

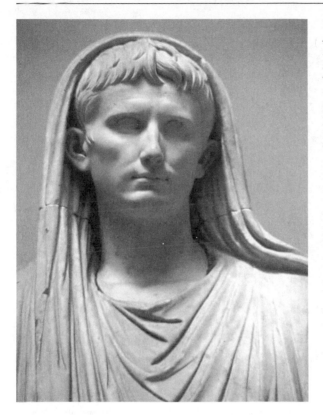

Figure 5.
Augustus after Becoming High Priest in 12 BCE.
This is a view of the head from a full-size statue of Augustus with his toga drawn over his head as when performing a sacrifice or in prayer. It is probably Augustus as *pontifex maximus* (high priest). There are numerous examples of Augustus "veiled with a toga" to emphasize his religious piety. *Museo Nazionale delle Terme, Rome.*

Photo from the Albert Hoxie Slide Collection, UCLA.

inspired or directed from Rome but was usually the result of local desire to honor, or flatter, Augustus (see Documents 22 and 24).

Although Augustus was not worshipped as a god in Rome during his lifetime, his deification of Caesar was a clear promise of his own future. And there were other indications. The *genius* (family spirit) of Augustus was worshipped in neighborhood shrines throughout Rome. The capital now had 265 *vici* (districts), each with an altar to the *Lares Augusti* (household gods of Augustus); fourteen of them survive. Even though the emperor was not a god in Rome, his deification at his death was expected.

Augustus, like Julius Caesar, was sympathetic to Jews in Rome and Judaea. He passed legislation to control anti-Jewish actions in Greek cities of Asia and Africa. And the Jews, alone among his subjects, were permitted to issue coinage without the emperor's portrait. Later Jewish

Figure 6.   *Gemma Augustea.*
In the symbolic top register of this cameo, Augustus sits as Jupiter next to the
goddess Roma. He is being crowned by Oecumene, the personification of the
entire world. On the left, Tiberius descends from the chariot while Germanicus stands armed next to Roma. On the ground to the right are the personifi-
cations of Italy and the Roman eagle. Above Augustus the solar disk completes
the cosmic order, smiling on the emperor. The lower register portrays Roman
troops and subjugated barbarians. *Kunsthistorisches Museum, Vienna.*
Erich Lessing/Art Resource, N.Y.

writers look back to the Augustan Age as a time of privilege and pro-
tection for the Jews (see Documents 36 and 37). Although Jesus
Christ was born in the time of Augustus, he was still a teenaged vil-
lage carpenter in Galilee when the emperor died (see Document 38).
His public life and execution took place entirely under the emperor
Tiberius.

THE ARMY IN WAR AND PEACE

War was central to the life and the public propaganda of Augustus for more than a half-century. From the teenager's first recruitment of troops in 44 BCE to the old man's traumatic loss of three legions in Germany in 9 CE, the *princeps* knew that above all else his power rested on the loyalty and effectiveness of his armies. While Cicero believed the center of Roman political life was the Senate and assembly, Augustus (like Caesar before him) understood that for a century the armies in the provinces had decided who would rule Rome. Yet Augustus' ambition was more than to gain and hold power; it was to create an effective government that would ensure Rome's permanent dominance over the Mediterranean world. Hence his desire for an Augustan Peace to satisfy the millions of Romans exhausted by the confiscations, proscriptions, destruction, and deprivation of decades of civil war. For the Romans, peace was the result of victory, conquest, and subjugation. There was no contradiction between the armed statue of Augustus and the Altar of Augustan Peace (see Figure 7). We see this dichotomy in the words of Virgil, where the task of Rome is "to impose a custom of peace, to spare the humbled, and crush the arrogant" (*Aeneid* VI 851).

When Augustus reduced his and Antony's sixty legions to twenty-eight, he had to provide over 100,000 men with the traditional form of pension—land. Many were settled in more than one hundred new colonies founded in Italy and throughout the provinces. These colonies, with a core of several thousand veterans and their families, became bulwarks of Roman domination in Europe, Africa, and Asia. Such modern cities as Barcelona and Zaragoza in Spain, Nîmes and Lyons in France, Turin in Italy, Tangiers in Morocco, Corinth in Greece, and Beirut in Lebanon all grew from Augustan colonies. They provided additional security in the provinces and eventually became important centers of Romanization.

In the civil wars republican armies had been armed and paid by the general who had recruited them. Most nobles served in the army as part of a senatorial career, but there were almost no career officers. Augustus professionalized his army by instituting a standard legionary command structure, ranks, and standard rates of pay. Annual pay ranged from 900 sesterces for a legionary to 15,000 sesterces for an ordinary centurion and 60,000 sesterces for a *primipilus* (the senior of the sixty centurions in a legion). This created an enormous incentive for soldiers to succeed and gain promotion.

Roman soldiers also swore an annual oath of loyalty to the emperor. To ensure that no rebellious general could threaten the regime, Augustus established a central military treasury and all the spoils of conquest flowed into it. He assured the legionaries they would receive a retirement grant after twenty years of service—usually equivalent to fourteen years' pay—to purchase land on which to support their families. Augustus made enormous payments from his booty from Egypt to establish the treasury for the first group of retirees after Actium. Later, to ensure future solvency, the emperor imposed a 5 percent death duty on large estates, as well as a 1 percent sales tax on all auctions; the proceeds of both went directly to the military treasury. Because this was the first direct taxation of Roman citizens in almost two centuries, there was some anger among the rich, but the emperor knew he must endure the grumbling. The soldiers received their pay, bonuses, and pensions from this central treasury, so there were few mutinies and legionaries were rarely tempted to follow a renegade commander.

Augustus also created more specialized army units. The more highly paid praetorian **cohorts** remained in Italy and were regarded as the personal guard of the emperor. Non-Romans were recruited to serve in auxiliary units that fought alongside the legions. Although they possessed skills that legionaries might have scorned—they included slingers from Majorca, archers from Syria, and cavalry from Gaul and Thrace—they permitted a more versatile fighting force. These men served longer and for lower pay than legionaries, but on their discharge they and their families were given Roman citizenship. Their citizen sons often served as legionaries. Thus the army became an engine of Romanization.

The civil wars had taught the value of maintaining a naval presence against an unexpected invasion, so naval bases were established in Ravenna and on the bay of Naples, to harbor fleets deployed to the east and west of Italy. Other small naval detachments served as far away as the Nile, to keep the seas clear of pirates for the increasing commercial activity. The ships were staffed by freedmen (former slaves) and noncitizens, who served under equestrian commanders.

After his defeat of Antony, Augustus was faced with the enormous tasks of organizing the eastern provinces and pacifying restive areas of Europe. In the East he adhered initially to the republican tradition of allowing client kings like Herod to administer their own territories, a policy that allowed Roman legions to be deployed elsewhere. Eventually, however, local dynastic squabbles led the emperor to annex eastern kingdoms such as Judaea, Armenia, and Galatia as Roman provinces. The royal estates in those areas then became the emperor's private property. Throughout the Empire, provinces with a large military presence—Spain, Syria, and Gaul—were retained by the emperor and governed by his deputies, while less strategic provinces with limited troops were ruled by senatorial proconsuls. The wealth of Egypt made it unique; it was governed by an equestrian prefect on behalf of the absent Pharaoh-emperor.

The emperor spent much time in the provinces directing military or diplomatic activities. After he completed the political arrangements of 27 BCE, the *princeps* was away from Rome for eight of the next fourteen years. For one with such fragile health, this absence was an indication of the extraordinary importance he attached to his travels. Republican proconsuls served far from Rome in their provinces, so Augustus' absence on campaign would have seemed normal to Romans. He spent 26–25 BCE in northern Spain, where he hoped finally to subdue the tenacious mountain peoples and gain access to their silver mines. Because he was ill during most of that campaign, he eventually declared victory and returned to Rome. A few years later, in 22 BCE, Augustus went to the East for three years. His main diplomatic agenda there was to negotiate with the Parthian king the return of Roman legionary standards lost by Crassus and Marc Antony (see cover photo). He also installed a pro-Roman king on the throne of Armenia. Although his successes at both Parthia and Armenia were represented in poetry, in art, and on Roman coins as great military victories, they were in fact the result of diplomatic pressure. After Augustus had spent three years back in Rome, German tribes crossed the Rhine into the Roman provinces in Gaul, forcing the emperor to leave for another three-year tour (16–13 BCE). His activities ranged from overseeing a Gallic census to supervising the activities of his stepsons Tiberius and Drusus along the Rhine and in the Alps. No one could accuse Augustus of being a remote ruler of his vast empire.

In 9 BCE, the imperial family witnessed the dedication of the Altar of Augustan Peace, on which they, along with senators and religious officials, were all portrayed (see Figure 7). Yet artistic paeans to peace should not delude us; Augustus was no pacifist.[11] The end of civil war also allowed Augustus to turn his attention to tribal incursions in the west. The Trophy of Augustus, which stands in the mountains high above Monaco, records his suppression of the stubborn Alpine tribes between Italy and France. Augustus also subdued northern Spain and extended Roman dominion to the Danube, where the new provinces

of Raetia, Noricum, Illyricum, Pannonia, and Moesia stretched from present Switzerland through Austria, Croatia, Serbia, and Hungary to Bulgaria on the Black Sea. He celebrated triumphs (and was called *imperator*) twenty-one times and, more important, brought more territory under Roman control than in any equivalent period in its history. In the East he was more cautious: He did not confront Rome's enemies in Parthia or Arabia, and he was wary of Nubia, to the south of Egypt.

The emperor's greatest military disaster came in Germany. In 9 BCE, Drusus marched across Germany as far as the Elbe and placed an altar to the emperor there (see Documents 30 and 31). Augustus believed that Germany was safely under Roman control. But seventeen years later, in 9 CE, his general Varus led three legions into annihilation in an ambush, a catastrophe—the worst Roman defeat in more than a century. (The site at Kalkreise was only confirmed by excavations through the 1990s—5,500 objects have now been found.)[12] Despite the devastating impact on the aged emperor, who we are told raged through the palace shouting "Varus, give me back my legions," he sent reinforcements and showed no intention to retreat from Germany.[13] That was only done by his successor, Tiberius. Augustus was forever regarded as a great conqueror who added to the territory and prosperity of the Roman state.

ITALY AND THE PROVINCES

The Italians had gained Roman citizenship in 88 BCE, but few had risen to positions of importance at Rome. Julius Caesar had shown great interest in the Italians, and even extended Roman citizenship to Gallic provincials living in the Po valley. When Augustus came to

---

Figure 7 (*Opposite*). *Ara Pacis Procession.*
On the occasion of Augustus' safe return to the city in 13 BCE after three years of campaigning in Gaul and Spain, the Senate voted for this Altar of Augustan Peace (*Ara Pacis*). The Altar, which was dedicated in 9 BCE, is surrounded by a wall covered with decorative reliefs. The side reliefs show senators, religious officials, and members of the imperial family in solemn procession. In this segment, after the priests with pointed hats and a lictor carrying the ceremonial axes of power, we have Agrippa and the empress Livia. The child between them could be Agrippa's seven-year-old son Gaius. This is the first official Roman procession to include women and children. *Ara Pacis, Rome.*
Alinari/Art Resource, N.Y.

power, Greek was still spoken in southern Italy and Gallic in the far north; Italic languages (Oscan and Umbrian) were spoken widely in mountain areas, and Etruscan had only recently died out. Augustus, whose own family originated outside Rome, understood that there was an enormous pool of unexploited talent residing in the cities of Italy. Throughout his reign, he promoted the integration of the Italian elite into Rome's own ruling class.

The emperor's closest personal friends and political allies, Marcus Agrippa and Gaius Maecenas, were such Italians. During the civil war, Octavian had attracted significant support from the Italian merchants and businessmen who feared Antony's victory might shift the economic center of the empire to Alexandria. Augustus was proud of these supporters. In his *Res Gestae* he boasted, "All Italy voluntarily swore an oath of allegiance to me," and in Virgil's *Aeneid* the scene on the shield of Aeneas depicts the Italians fighting for Augustus at Actium (see Document 48). The economic boom that followed the long civil wars enriched the towns and drew Italy together. It was Augustus, then, who truly achieved the cultural, political, and economic unification of ancient Italy (see Figure 8).

The new regime used Cleopatra's treasure to launch a great building program and also to reward its loyal supporters. Augustus' overwhelming wealth allowed him to become the patron of all Roman citizens, and in keeping with Roman tradition, he could expect loyalty from his clients. The emperor built the useful (roads, bridges, and aqueducts) and the ornamental (triumphal arches, temples, and baths) throughout the peninsula. New colonies in the north promoted Latinization so that for the first time in its history Italy became culturally and linguistically united. Many Italians of the local elite now became senators. In a striking irony, the consul of 9 CE came from the same family as the Samnite rebel of 90 BCE who was "consul" of the Italian forces against Rome in the Social War. This increasing union of

---

Figure 8 (*Opposite*).   *Mother Earth on Ara Pacis, 9 BCE.*
This image of a goddess of abundance has been variously identified as *Terra Mater* (Mother Earth), Italy, Venus, and Peace. No one can be certain, but the cornucopia of fruits in her lap and plants behind her, the two babies, and the animals at her feet seem to convey the fertility bestowed on Italy by the mother goddess. This fertility is a recurring theme in Augustan literature. *Ara Pacis, Rome.*
Nimitallah/Art Resource, N.Y.

Romans and Italians allowed Augustus to recruit from an expanding pool of talent to govern the Empire.

Augustus took a different view of his role from earlier Roman politicians: he was not just the ruler of a city-state that happened to rule the world; he was the emperor of a vast, multicultural world empire whose capital was at Rome. Roman colonies brought Roman citizens and Roman culture to the provinces, while provincials who served in the armies might become citizens themselves. The census results reported in the *Res Gestae* show an increase from about four million to five million citizens (out of a total population of sixty million) during the reign of the first emperor. Augustus brought more citizens into the administration of the Empire than had ever been the case under the Republic.

For sixty years, the eastern provinces had been a battleground between Roman factions. Roman generals had confiscated temple treasures and imposed irregular taxes on the population to pay their troops. Sulla, Pompey, Caesar, Brutus, and Antony all pillaged the Greek cities of Europe and Asia. Now Augustus had to restore political and economic order. If Brutus had demanded and collected ten years' of taxes (in advance) from certain cities, how would Augustus take account of those payments? The emperor's eastern expert, Agrippa, spent many years traveling from city to city, establishing new institutions, and between 22 and 19 BCE the emperor himself remained in the east. Augustus visited dozens of cities in Greece and Asia and directed diplomatic efforts, resulting in peace with Parthia. This hands-on administration was the way in which Augustus made a genuine empire out of what had been a group of provinces (see Document 33). The restoration of orderly government was hard work, but it was appreciated, as we can see from the enthusiasm of Greek writers like Dionysius and Strabo for the new regime.

The imperial administration was more efficient and more welcome to the locals than republican administration—even Tacitus admitted that (see Document 32)! The provinces fared better than they had under the corrupt governors and rapacious tax collectors of the Republic. Augustus did not have a clear plan—except in Egypt—but he brought a sensible flexibility and, to be sure, a certain opportunism to his arrangements. He did not like Herod, who had been Antony's ally, but the emperor saw that Herod kept Judaea under control without Roman troops, so he kept Herod in place while he removed the king of Galatia and made that land a province. Some provinces, like Gaul and Asia, established "councils" at which representatives of the cities assembled annually to consult with the Roman governor, but most prov-

Figure 9. *Bust of Livia, about 25 BCE.*

Busts of the wife of Augustus and the mother of the second emperor, Tiberius, were common throughout the empire. Although Augustus married her while she was pregnant with her first husband's son, he launched a campaign of moral reform. The sources show the deep ambivalence of the Romans to seeing a woman in a position of great power. This statue of young Livia was found in Egypt. *Ny Carlsberg Glypotek, Copenhagen.*

Photo from the Albert Hoxie Slide Collection, UCLA.

inces did not. In all, the emperor succeeded in bringing to most of the provinces a stability they had not seen since Rome's domestic civil wars spilled across the Mediterranean. When cities honored Augustus as a living god and a savior, they had good reason to do so.

THE IMPERIAL FAMILY AND SUCCESSION

In 40 BCE, while he was maneuvering to secure support against Antony, Octavian entered a politically useful marriage with the much older Scribonia. But in January 38 BCE, barely waiting for the birth of their only child, Julia, he divorced his wife and married the beautiful Livia Drusilla, who belonged to the distinguished Claudian family (Figure 9). Livia had given birth to one son, Tiberius, and at the time of the marriage was pregnant with a second, Drusus, by her first husband. Even the ancient writers, who believed that Augustus was notoriously calculating, recognized that this was a marriage of love and passion. Although the couple never had children, Livia remained at her husband's side as he traveled across the Empire and was certainly his closest advisor (see Document 42).

After 27 BCE, Augustus began to think of his successor (Figure 10). In many ways the succession was the most difficult problem Augustus ever faced, one that caused him considerable heartbreak. Some of that was of his own creation. Because he had reached power through his adoption by Caesar, he could never shake a belief that the political legitimacy of the regime (and the loyalty of the army) depended on his choosing a blood relative as a successor. Rather than choosing to designate his daughter Julia's sons as his successors when they were children, he might have designated Agrippa, Drusus, or Tiberius, who were far more competent to govern. But he could not break free of the dynastic model.

Augustus certainly did not wish to see Rome descend again into civil war. Because his health was never very strong, the absence of a designated successor might encourage opposition if he became seriously ill. In 25 BCE, he married Julia to his nephew Marcellus, who was popular with the people and liked by the *princeps* himself. When Augustus became seriously ill in 23 BCE, however, he recognized that at nineteen years old Marcellus was still too young to govern, and he gave his signet ring instead to his old friend Agrippa (see Document 13). When Marcellus died later in the same year, Agrippa divorced his wife and married Julia. The couple had five children—the only grandchildren of Augustus (see Document 39).

The first grandsons, Gaius (born in 20 BCE) and Lucius (17 BCE), became the focus of the emperor's emotional and political hopes. He adopted them as his sons and carefully directed their education (see Document 41). As republican senators had done with their sons, Augustus took them to meetings and on his travels so that they might learn to govern. Although he still had Agrippa and Livia's sons Tiberius and Drusus to lead armies and administer difficult provinces, the honors he bestowed on Gaius and Lucius showed where the succession lay (see Document 40). But the unexpected death of Agrippa in 12 BCE removed not only the emperor's most faithful friend but the boys' guardian if Augustus were to die.

The emperor moved quickly and ruthlessly. Tiberius was forced to divorce his much-loved wife to marry the widowed Julia; it was a marriage that brought misery to the entire family. The boys survived—at least for a time. In 5 BCE, Augustus assumed the consulship for the first time since 23 CE, so he could present his fifteen-year-old grandson Gaius with the man's toga and designate him to become consul at

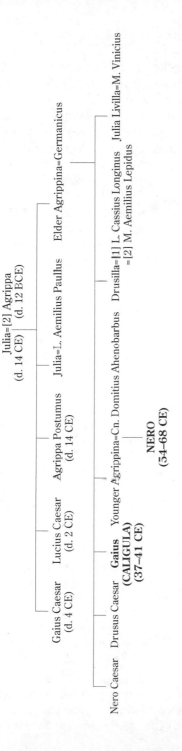

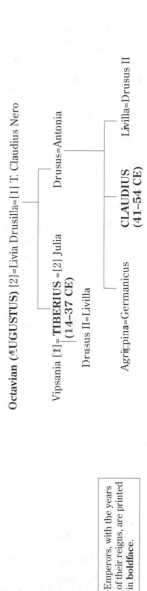

Figure 10. *Genealogy of the Descendants of Augustus and Livia.*
Illustration created by Ronald Mellor.

the age of twenty. Three years later he did the same for Lucius. These were the only times in the last thirty-seven years of his life that Augustus allowed himself to be elected to the consulship. The boys were now men; a bitter Tiberius, trapped in an unhappy marriage, understood that he was dispensable and withdrew into voluntary exile on the island of Rhodes in 6 BCE. When Augustus learned of Julia's many love affairs in 2 BCE, she was exiled for life to a small island. There is more than a suspicion that she had become entangled in a political conspiracy, but the sources are vague.

There was no happy ending for the emperor. Lucius died in 2 CE on his way to Spain; two years later, Gaius, after being wounded on an eastern campaign, died at age twenty-three. Two other grandchildren were exiled: Agrippa Postumus for his violent disposition and the younger Julia for adultery (like her mother). Of the five grandchildren, only young Agrippina kept Augustus' line alive.

Augustus then turned to his moody stepson, Tiberius, whom he adopted in 4 CE. Tiberius served as co-regent for the next decade. Augustus was fortunate to have him; Tiberius put down rebellions along the Danube and, after the disaster of Varus, secured the Rhine frontier as well. He served the emperor remarkably well, but even at the end Tiberius was a pawn in the emperor's dynastic ambitions (see Document 43). He was forced to adopt as his own heir his nephew Germanicus, who was married to Augustus' granddaughter Agrippina. This was to ensure that blood heirs of Augustus would eventually reach the throne. Only two of them did; we know them as Caligula and Nero.

Despite four decades of intrigue and disaster, the succession in 14 CE was smooth (see Document 54). The power Augustus had granted Tiberius was confirmed by a vote of the Senate and the first imperial transition had taken place. Livia saw her son become emperor, and lived fifteen years longer. At her death at the age of 89 in 29 CE, Livia Drusilla, now called Augusta, was one of the few survivors who had seen the Republic, the age of Caesar and the triumvirs, and sixty years of Empire. She too became a goddess.

"A CITY OF MARBLE"

Augustus boasted that he found Rome "a city of brick and left it a city of marble." Of course there had been major building projects all through the Republic with architects drawing on Etruscan and Greek models. The Romans had previously imported some expensive marble from Greece, but they usually used brick and local limestone. To transform Rome into the true cosmopolitan capital of the Mediterranean world, however, Augustus had to compete with the architectural marvels of Athens, Pergamum, and Alexandria. He was able to exploit newly discovered quarries of gleaming white marble at Carrara in northern Italy to adorn Rome with splendid buildings (see Documents 50, 51, and 52).[14]

Since the Roman Forum was no longer adequate for the commercial and political demands of a growing empire, Augustus added the adjoining Forum of Augustus (see Figure 11), which was dedicated in 2 BCE. There sculptors and architects took Greek columns and capitals and transformed them into a distinctly Roman architectural setting. They decorated it with statues and inscriptions honoring great Romans of the past, like Romulus, the founder of Rome, along with the emperor's "ancestors" from the Julian family, most notably Aeneas. Artists and architects in the ancient world required wealthy patrons, and their work inevitably reflected the desires of those who paid for the work.

Augustus decided to make the Campus Martius—the flat open area once used for military exercises—the focus of his building. There, beside the Tiber, he created a beautiful suburb. His large family tomb, built in 28 BCE as the Mausoleum of Augustus, still stands today. It once formed part of a complex that included a massive sundial with an obelisk brought from Egypt serving as the pointer (Figure 12), as well as the Altar of Augustan Peace. The enclosure wall bears mythic scenes of Aeneas, Mars, and Venus, with an emphasis on the prosperity and tranquility of Rome under the new regime. Although carved by Greek craftsmen, its themes are purely Roman and Augustan: myth, family, fertility (see Figure 8), and religious devotion. The gods on either end flank processions of senators and the entire imperial family, children and all (see Figure 7).

But not all of Augustus' urban improvements were overtly political. His son-in-law Agrippa filled the city with new porticos, baths, and temples, and he improved the system of aqueducts to bring water to Rome and other cities of the Empire. This building program provided work to the citizens, spacious public amenities, and the beautification of the city. The emperor also introduced police and fire protection to Rome—security ensured by the praetorian cohorts and the first public fire department of 7,000 freedmen commanded by a prefect.

More busts of Augustus than of any other Roman appeared throughout the Empire in public spaces and private homes. Yet the emperor himself, ostentatiously unostentatious, lived in a modest house on

Figure 11. *Forum of Augustus: Reconstructed Model.*

Before the battle of Philippi, Octavian vowed to build a temple to Mars the Avenger if he were victorious. About forty years later, in 2 BCE, he dedicated this imposing temple as the centerpiece of his new Forum. The temple, regarded by Pliny as one of the most beautiful buildings in the world, contained cult statues of Mars, Venus, and the deified Julius Caesar. Sculptures in the side colonnades depicted Julius Caesar's ancestors, like Aeneas, as well as Roman heroes of the past. *Museo della Civiltà Romana, Rome.*

Alinari/Art Resource, N.Y.

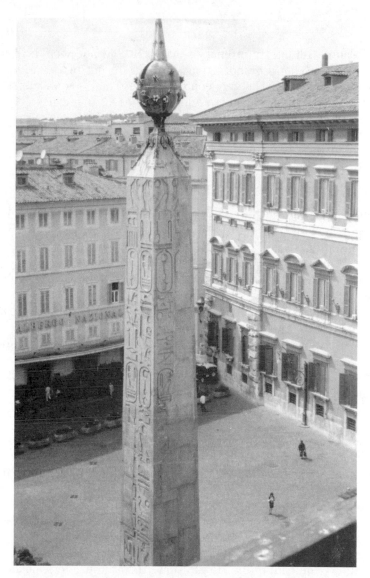

Figure 12. *Obelisk in Piazza del Montecitorio.*
This obelisk was originally erected in Egypt in the sixth century BCE and was brought to Rome by Augustus. In 10 BCE, the emperor set it up as the pointer of an enormous sundial—the largest in the world—and dedicated it to the Roman god of the sun. It stood for over a thousand years before it collapsed. In the eighteenth century, it was re-erected at its current location in front of what is now the Italian parliament. *Piazza del Montecitorio, Rome.*
Photo by Tristan Shamp.

the Palatine Hill like an ordinary senator. He did not need, or desire, the reassurance of a grand setting, nor did he put his name on the temples he rebuilt. He was content to see that his theaters and temples, his aqueducts and triumphal arches changed not only the face of Rome but the entire Empire. They are testaments to his generosity, his political shrewdness, and his good taste.

THE GOLDEN AGE OF LATIN LITERATURE

At the end of the Republic, Latin literature was barely two centuries old, and its few poetic masterpieces had relied heavily on Greek models. During the first century BCE, numerous Roman intellectuals like Caesar, Cicero, and Horace travelled east to study Greek poetry and rhetoric in Athens and Rhodes. The Roman elite now spoke Greek fluently and often had Greeks in their households at Rome. The growth of Roman literary and cultural Hellenization was in full force just as the Republic collapsed.

Under Augustus, writers from all parts of Italy journeyed to Rome, where, as in Periclean Athens and Elizabethan England, generous patronage and the self-confidence born of military success propelled them to extraordinary achievements. Most hailed the arrival of a new Golden Age, which Horace explicitly called the age of Augustus (*Odes* 4, 15: *your age, Caesar*) (see Document 47). Augustus' friend and policy advisor, Maecenas, found and subsidized the most creative and sophisticated poets Rome had yet produced. They were not paid to write propaganda, but most shared the emperor's vision of a return to traditional Roman values.

Livy, from Padua in northern Italy, wrote a history of Rome from mythic times to his own day, in 142 books. Only a quarter of the enormous work has survived. His stirring accounts of Rome's early struggle for freedom (the rape of Lucretia, the expulsion of the Tarquin kings, the oath of the Horatii) have inspired painters, poets, and political leaders through the centuries. Livy was so deeply devoted to the old Republic that his friend Augustus publicly teased him as a "Pompeian." The man was above all a moralist who used history to illustrate the virtues that brought Rome greatness.

Horace's diverse collection of poems, the *Odes,* drew on Greek poetry in praising love, wine, and the simple life of the countryside. His six "Roman Odes" exalt the political achievements of his patron Augustus, while his *Satires* shows a genial wit, as in the fable of the city mouse and the country mouse. He had become close enough to the emperor to address an *Epistle* directly to him. Horace predicted the eternity of the Roman people and his own work: "I will not entirely die, since my poetry is a monument more lasting than bronze."

The greatest Roman poet, Virgil, born on a farm near Mantua, witnessed Octavian's early confiscations, but he later joined the imperial circle. His early work, *Eclogues,* contained elegant adaptations of Greek poems set among shepherds, but in his later *Georgics,* at his patron Maecenas' suggestion, he turned to the more patriotic theme of the beauty of the Italian countryside. These poems, written during the struggle against Antony, used the revival of agriculture to symbolize the moral and economic rebirth of Italy under Augustus. His central theme of order brought out of chaos would continue into the *Aeneid.*

Virgil modeled his masterpiece, the *Aeneid,* on Homer's *Iliad* and *Odyssey.* In this patriotic epic of duty and sacrifice, the hero Aeneas, a mythical ancestor of Augustus, abandons his great love, Queen Dido of Carthage, to search for an Italian homeland and found the Roman people. The poem is a testimony to the values of the Augustan age: imperial spirit, the power of destiny and renunciation, the necessity for struggle, and the pathos of loss. Aeneas sacrifices love and human compassion on the altar of duty and conquest, demonstrating that every great victory, every noble achievement entails a cost, and his melancholy stems from a deep appreciation of what has been lost. Virgil had not completed the poem when he died in 19 BCE, and Augustus personally countermanded the poet's dying request that the manuscript be burned.

Not every Augustan poet was so serious, nor did they all treat grand themes. Propertius of Assisi was an ardent poet of love and sexual passion who politely avoided war and politics in his elegies. For the urbane and irreverent Ovid from Sulmona in central Italy, love was above all a game. His *Art of Love* is a handbook of sex and seduction for both men and women, its contents ranging from cosmetics to pickup techniques at the chariot races. Ovid's masterpiece was the *Metamorphoses,* an enormous poem in which he turns his sophisticated wit to a series of tales from Greek mythology. Some regard it as a "counter-epic"—an antidote to the seriousness of the *Aeneid.* The poet's story of the sculptor Pygmalion, who falls in love with his own statue, was later retold in the musical comedy *My Fair Lady,* in which Professor Henry Higgins transforms the lowly Eliza Doolittle into a "lady." Late in the reign of Augustus, Ovid became involved in some mysterious scandal that caused his banishment to a small town on the Black Sea. The sophisticated poet was miserable living at the edge of the known world, and wrote letters to the emperor begging for pardon. But he was never forgiven; he died in wretched exile, guilty, he said, of "a poem and a mistake." Scholars still dispute exactly what he did to so infuriate Augustus, although the best guess may be a tasteless poem about the emperor's adulterous daughter, Julia.

Virgil, Horace, Ovid, Propertius, and Livy were all closely linked to the emperor. Although poets often flatter their patrons with allusions to a Golden Age, the work of these writers is evidence of the brilliance of the cultural revival. Horace says that "Caesar could compel them," but there was no need. These nonpolitical Italians, who had made their way to Rome in the aftermath of civil war, loved the countryside, loved Rome, and loved the Empire. Nearly all sincerely admired the new regime and its achievements (see Document 49). Because they had lived through the civil wars, their praise of the Augustan peace was not mere propaganda. But writing over nearly half a century, these poets were not monolithic in their interests. In addition to the achievements of Rome, they also celebrated many aspects of the human condition. It is no small accomplishment when a politician befriends such a collection of writers and fosters their genius. For his poets alone, Augustus merits the claim of having inspired a Golden Age.

THE DEATH AND LEGACY OF AUGUSTUS

The very name Caesar Augustus has echoed down through the centuries. The emperor's successors at Rome usually adopted his names and titles; even the modern titles of tsar, emperor, and kaiser hark back to his illustrious reign. For two millennia, kings and emperors, princes and popes have lived in palaces, which take their name from Augustus' residence on the Palatine Hill. Ironically, however, Augustus' name has been disseminated most widely in a passage written by a Jewish Christian in Greek. The second chapter of the gospel attributed to St. Luke reads, "At that time it came to pass that a decree went out from Caesar Augustus, that the whole world should be registered" (see Document 38). Even humble people in distant provinces knew that the immense power of the Roman emperor could affect their everyday lives.

Augustus was not a military genius, but he was a brilliant politician. After his allies and generals defeated Brutus and Cassius, Sextus Pompey and Lepidus, Antony and Cleopatra, his task was to create a new, stable constitution. From the institutions and traditional rhetoric of the past he wove a completely new system of government that would last for centuries. It was a remarkable mix of tradition and innovation.

While Augustus presented himself as a proponent of Roman traditions, he adhered to the past only in his reconstruction of Roman society. In politics, he was in fact a revolutionary. His was a broader vision that went far beyond that of the senatorial elite. He restored loyalty to the state among the armies, the masses, and the Italians. He created new forms of administration to bring a more benign rule to the sixty million people living under Roman rule.

The historian Tacitus said that Augustus "had seduced the soldiers with bonuses, the people with food, and everyone with the sweetness of peace" (see Document 7). And so he had. For senators like Tacitus, writing a century later, the loss of liberty seemed too great a price to pay for relief from the horrors of civil war. But the "liberty" of the late Republic had allowed a few hundred men to divide the offices and spoils of the Empire, while the plebeians and the provincials paid the price of conquest. Most groups found the loss of "liberty" a cheap price to pay for peace and stability.

Although the Augustan Peace brought social stability, economic revival, and efficient administration, it did not ensure Rome's future. Ostensibly Augustus owed his power to the Senate and Roman people, but his position was in fact personal, and his death might bring a renewal of civil war. Was it only one man's longevity that allowed the Roman state to survive in a new form? For decades, Augustus watched his chosen successors die, until only his stepson Tiberius remained. Combining birth with adoption, Augustus set the precedent that his successors would follow. Struggles for power that were once fought on the battlefield would now be waged in the private rooms of the imperial palace.

On his deathbed in 14 CE, at the age of seventy-five, Augustus asked if he had played his part well in the *mimus vitae*—the comedy of life (see Documents 53 and 54). He added a curtain line from a Greek comedy, asking that the audience applaud (for Augustus' sense of humor, see Document 15). He had certainly played many roles well: the respectful heir of Caesar, the ruthless young murderer of the purges, the priggish moralist against Antony, the astute politician of the reconstruction, and the patron of literature and art. In the end, he came to be seen as the beneficent father figure who provided food, entertainment, and peace to the Roman people. The Greeks had called Augustus a god in his lifetime; at his death he was deified in Rome (see Figure 6). In an age in which cities generously called their benefactors "saviors" and "gods," Augustus above all others deserved to be called Savior of the Roman people.

THE EVALUATION OF AUGUSTUS

The evaluation of Augustus has posed problems for historians from antiquity to modern times.[15] When Tacitus wrote of the emperor's funeral, he staged a fictitious debate in which Romans praise and condemn Augustus (see Document 55). For centuries, the emperor was seen as the founder of a great empire that endured in Rome until 476 CE and in Constantinople until 1453 CE. Several kings in France and Germany took "Augustus" as one of their names. In the late nineteenth and early twentieth centuries, Augustus was seen as a benevolent and compassionate ruler—an image that appears in the early 1930s in the first edition of the *Cambridge Ancient History*. In the decades that followed, however, many historians became suspicious of "strong" leaders and "great" men, seeing their potential to become despots and do great harm. Some scholars even saw Augustus as a leader of a political gang—a precursor of the thuggish European despots of that time, Hitler, Mussolini, and Stalin—believing that like them he disguised his coup d'état behind a façade of constitutional artifice and propaganda. Yet others believed that without Augustus the Roman state would have collapsed and Mediterranean and European history would have been dramatically different. Scholars have debated and continue to debate the contributions of Caesar Augustus.

Why is the evidence so contradictory? Many sources have been lost, especially those of the republicans and of Marc Antony's supporters. There was a hysterical propaganda war in the 30s BCE, and the personal attacks obscured policy differences. Most of all, the remarkable length of Augustus' public life—almost sixty years—encompassed widely varying circumstances. Anyone can appear gentler in time of peace than during a vicious civil war.

Augustus was not a typical autocrat. He was not a general, an orator, or an intellectual or a religious leader. Certain character traits are clear, however. Augustus had courage, intelligence, and charisma. He gave loyal support to his friends, and could retain the loyalty of others. He could take a joke—even one aimed at himself—and had an amiable manner that disarmed his opponents. As a triumvir he was certainly brutal. Although there was no modern police state, he sent thousands to their deaths in the proscriptions, killed his prisoners in the Perusine War, and even murdered Caesar's own son, Caesarion. After 27 BCE, as Tacitus said, however, he preferred to seduce his opponents. In the forty-five years after he came to absolute power at Actium, he seems to have killed no more than a few hundred Romans.

While that is terrible in itself, it is far less brutal than other absolute rulers. He was indeed a monarch, but one who did not act like a king. Augustus cared deeply about the governing of the Roman Empire; even in old age he worked hard, hearing law cases and making public appearances (see Documents 56–59).

In what ways did Augustus reinforce or transform Roman institutions? He preserved the social hierarchy and the tradition of using local elites to administer the Empire. He restored the rule of law, which had collapsed during the turbulent decades of civil war. He professionalized the Roman army, making it the chief mechanism of social mobility and Romanization in the provinces. In rendering the ideology of monarchic rule, in a carefully sweetened form, acceptable to the Roman people for the first time in five centuries, Augustus provided a means for the transmission of power without using the word "king." And not least, he made the city of Rome worthy of being the capital of the world's greatest Empire.

It is not just that the evidence is contradictory; Augustus himself was full of contradictions. He murdered Cicero but later praised him sentimentally as "one who loved his country." Was that hypocrisy, or was it a ruthless and cagey judgment about political necessity? Did he destroy the freedom of the Roman Republic or save the state from the self-regarding senatorial elite? The emperor himself acknowledged these contradictions when he chose the sphinx—the symbol of obscurity—for his signet ring. Regardless, we can recognize the results of his years in power. He accomplished the enormous political task of restoring the Roman state. His success can be measured by the fact that in the two centuries between Actium in 31 BCE and the death of Marcus Aurelius in 180 CE there was a single year of civil war (69 CE), and only about twenty-five years of overt tyranny. The Augustan Peace had brought an extraordinary period of stability. That stability allowed the Greco-Roman cultural synthesis to solidify and to plant its linguistic, religious, and institutional roots throughout western Europe, where they continue to endure. That is no small legacy for any leader.

NOTES

[1]K. Hopkins, "Conquerers and Slaves: The Impact of Conquering an Empire on the Political Economy of Italy," in *Conquerers and Slaves: Sociological Studies in Roman History* (Cambridge: Cambridge University Press, 1978), 1–98.

[2]This image of Roman agriculture, which goes back to Appian's *Civil War*, 1, 7–10, perhaps relied too heavily on Gaius Gracchus' self-serving biography of his brother. That view was widely accepted by many scholars, although there have been recent arguments in favor of the continuity of the free peasantry. See J. K. Evans, "Plebs Restica," *American Journal of Ancient History*, 5 (1980): 19–47; 134–73; S. Dyson, *Community and Society in Roman Italy* (Baltimore: Johns Hopkins University Press, 1992).

[3]For another perspective on recruitment, see J. Rich, "The Supposed Roman Manpower Shortage in the Later Second Century BC," *Historia*, 32 (1983): 287–331.

[4]E. Gabba, *Republican Rome, the Army and the Allies* (Berkeley: University of California Press, 1976), 1–52, traced the development of the professional army down to Augustus.

[5]K. Hopkins and G. Burton, "Political Succession in the Late Republic (249–50 BC)," in K. Hopkins, *Death and Renewal* (Cambridge: Cambridge University Press, 1983), 31–119, prove a detailed statistical and demographic study of senatorial competition for high office.

[6]For a readable biography of Julius Caesar, see Christian Meier, *Caesar* (New York: Basic Books, 1982). Plutarch has provided ancient biographies of all three triumvirs.

[7]N. Lewis, *Life in Egypt Under Roman Rule* (Oxford: Oxford University Press, 1983), 15. Scholars differ on the consumption of grain at Rome and how much came from Egypt. P. Garnsey, "Grain for Rome," in P. Garnsey, K. Hopkins, and R. Whittaker, *Trade in the Ancient Economy* (London: Chatto and Windus, 1983), 118, also posits a consumption of 200,000 tons and provides calculations.

[8]J. Linderski, "Mommsen and Syme: Law and Power in the Principate of Augustus," in K. Raaflaub and M. Toher, *Between Republic and Empire: Interpretations of Augustus and His Principate* (Berkeley: University of California Press, 1990), 42–53.

[9]R. Syme, *The Roman Revolution* (Oxford: Clarendon Press, 1939). See also G. Alföldy, "Two Principes: Augustus and Sir Ronald Syme," *Athenaeum*, 81 (1993): 101–22. This is a text of the first Ronald Syme Lecture delivered at Wolfson College in 1991. For other essays on Syme's impact, see H. Galsterer, "A Man, a Book, and a Method: Sir Ronald Syme's *Roman Revolution* after Fifty Years," and Z. Yavetz, "The Personality of Augustus: Reflections on Syme's *Roman Revolution*," both in Raaflaub and Toher (see n. 8).

[10]For a recent survey of imperial finances and taxation, see D. W. Rathbone, "The Imperial Finances," in *The Cambridge Ancient History*, vol. X, *The Augustan Empire, 43 B.C.–A.D. 69*, 2nd ed., ed. A. K. Bowman, E. Champlin, and A. Lintott (Cambridge: Cambridge University Press, 1996), 309–23; A. K. Bowman, "Provincial Administration and Taxation," Ibid., 344–70.

[11]On the campaigns of Augustus, see also E. Gruen, "The Imperial Policy of Augustus," in Raaflaub and Toher (see n. 8), 395–416.

[12]On the archaeological discoveries at Kalkreise, see W. Schlüter, "The Battle of the Teutoburg Forest: Archaeological Research at Kalkreise near Osnabrück," in J. D. Creighton and R. J. A. Wilson, "Roman Germany: Studies in Cultural Interaction," *Journal of Roman Archaeology*, Suppl. 32 (1999): 125–59. See also Peter Wells, *The Battle That Stopped Rome: Emperor Augustus, Arminius, and the Slaughter of the Legions in the Teutoburg Forest* (Princeton: Princeton University Press, 2003).

[13]On Augustus' military reactions to the disaster, see E. Gruen, "The Expansion of the Empire under Augustus," in *Cambridge Ancient History*, vol. X (see n. 10), 148–98; on Germany, especially 178–88.

[14]The classic assessment of Augustus' building program remains P. Zanker, *The Power of Images in the Age of Augustus*, trans. A. Shapiro (Ann Arbor: University of Michigan Press, 1988).

[15]See D. Stockton, "Augustus *Sub Specie Aeternitatis*," *Thought*, 55 (1980): 5–17.

Principal Literary Sources
for the Age of Augustus

Although some of the evidence for Augustus are the inscriptions and sculpture carved on stone during his reign, the bulk of our knowledge comes from writers—historians, biographers, and poets. A few poets wrote while Augustus was alive, but nearly all historical accounts come from writers who lived a century or more after the emperor's death. It is important to situate these sources in their own historical context.

Appian (ca. 95–160s CE) Appian was a Greek born in Alexandria in Egypt. He became a Roman citizen and came to Rome to plead legal cases. He was appointed an imperial procurator on the recommendation of the famous advocate (and imperial tutor) Fronto. His *Romaika* (*Roman History*) was organized around the wars the Romans fought in their rise to greatness, such as Spanish Wars, Hannibalic Wars, Syrian Wars. About ten of the twenty-four books survive. The *Civil Wars* survives in five books, beginning with Tiberius Gracchus in 133 BCE and ending in 35 BCE. (The lost books on the *Egyptian Wars* dealt with Augustus' confrontation with Antony and Cleopatra.) Although he wrote almost two centuries after the events, Appian used Augustus' lost *Autobiography* as well as now-lost histories sympathetic to Marc Antony.

Aulus Gellius (ca. 125–180s CE) Gellius worked as a lawyer and judge, but his great passion was reading and antiquarian scholarship. His *Attic Nights* in twenty books is a compendium of notes of his reading, and fragments of grammar, philosophy, and law that he had collected. Like other writers of the second century, he preferred the archaic style and so collected passages of early Roman writers, such as Cato the Elder, who might otherwise be lost.

Cassius Dio (ca. 164–230s CE) Cassius Dio was a wealthy Greek from the city of Nicaea in Asia Minor (today Iznik in Turkey, across the Bosporos from Istanbul). His father was consul, so the teenaged Dio visited Rome by about 180 CE and within a decade had become **quaestor**

and a member of the Senate. His career progressed under the Severan emperors and he twice held the consulship, as well as important governorships. He wrote a *Roman History* in eighty books; some books survive intact while of others we have only summaries or excerpts. His account of the age of Augustus is the most extensive that has survived. His position at the Severan court made him sympathetic to imperial power, although he is at times critical of Augustus.

Marcus Tullius Cicero (106–43 BCE)   Cicero was the greatest orator of ancient Rome as well as an important politician of the late Republic. He was an early supporter of Pompey the Great and felt betrayed when Pompey joined Caesar in the First Triumvirate. Although he was not part of the conspiracy against Caesar—Brutus may have thought he talked too much and wrote too many letters—he was sympathetic to the assassins.

In addition to speeches and books on religion, rhetoric, government, and philosophy, Cicero wrote numerous letters, of which nine hundred survive. These are real letters; he was not thinking of their publication. So they often reveal his ambivalence and confusion in the face of political transformations. During the months after the Ides of March, he allowed his vanity to be flattered by Octavian. It cost him dearly; he was murdered in Antony and Octavian's proscriptions on December 7, 43 BCE.

Dionysius of Halicarnassus   Dionysius was a Greek orator from Halicarnassus in Asia Minor who came to Rome in 30 BCE to teach rhetoric. His *Roman Antiquities* covers the history of Rome from the beginnings to 264 BCE.

Gaius (flourished 160 CE)   Gaius received his legal training in Rome, but he delivered lectures at the law school in the Roman colony of Berytus (modern Beirut) in 160 CE. He wrote a number of scholarly books on the law, but he is most famous for his introductory textbook, *The Institutes.* That book developed classifications of law followed by later Roman writers and used into modern times by European scholars of civil law (which follows Roman law).

Horace (65–8 BCE)   Horace was the son of a southern Italian freedman, who as a young man fought with the republican forces at Philippi. He was later introduced by Virgil to Maecenas, who provided him with a Sabine farm and the leisure to write. He was drawn into the circle of the emperor and became a personal friend of Augustus. His lyric poems—four books of *Odes*—present Roman themes in Greek poetic forms. The poems concern love, wine, and the countryside, as well as the traditional Roman values that Augustus wished to promote. Other poems include *Satires* and *Epistles,* which includes the famous *Art of Poetry,* which had lasting influence on later European writers.

Josephus (37–ca. 100 CE)   The Jewish aristocrat Josephus was the commander of the rebel army in Galilee during the Great Revolt. He was captured by the Romans and became part of the general Vespasian's entourage. When Vespasian returned to Rome as emperor, Josephus accompanied him and wrote his eyewitness account, *The Jewish War,* first in Aramaic and then translated into Greek. He then began his *Jewish Antiquities*—a history of the Jewish people from the Creation until the outbreak of the Jewish Revolt in 66 CE. Although he became pro-Roman, Josephus remained a defender of Jewish culture and tradition and tried to explain them (in Greek) to the Greeks and Romans. He also wrote his autobiography and *Against Apion,* which defends the Jews against anti-Semitic Greeks.

Macrobius (born ca. 390 CE)   Ambrosius Theodosius Macrobius had a brilliant administrative career early in the fifth century CE. Although scholars have identified him with several political figures, he seems most likely to have been the praetorian prefect for Italy in 430. He wrote a commentary on Cicero's *Dream of Cicero,* but Macrobius' great work is his *Saturnalia*—one of the very last works of Roman paganism in a Christian empire. The book is a series of learned dialogues on religion, philosophy, ancient humor, and especially Virgil. Although Macrobius took material from a wide range of Greek and Latin sources, he brought his material together in a coherent work.

Nicolaus of Damascus (64 BCE–ca. 6 CE)   Nicolaus was highly educated in the Greek tradition and became a philosopher. He was a close advisor to Herod, for whom he undertook diplomatic missions to Rome. He also served as tutor to the surviving children of Antony and Cleopatra when they were brought to Rome after Actium. He wrote the enormous *Universal History* in 144 books, known only through excerpts, and a short panegyric, *Life of Augustus.*

Ovid (43 BCE–17 CE)   Ovid was the third of the great Augustan poets and, like Virgil and Horace, he was Italian in origin. He was a far less serious poet, and his urbane wit appears in his love poems (*Amores*), in his parodies of didactic poems (*Art of Love; Remedy for Love*), and in his great *Metamorphoses.* The *Metamorphoses* is the most comprehensive treatment of ancient mythology in Latin, and it was for the Renaissance the source of many Greek myths. He deeply offended Augustus and was forced to pass his last nine years in miserable exile on the shore of the Black Sea.

Philo (ca. 25 BCE–ca. 40s CE)   The philosopher Philo was one of the leaders of the Jewish community in Alexandria. He had a Greek education, but because he used the Greek translation of the Bible, it is uncertain whether he knew Hebrew. His writings had a great effect on both pagan and Christian Neoplatonic philosophers. Some relatives married into the Jewish royal family, while his nephew Tiberius Julius Alexander became prefect of Egypt. In 39 CE, as an old man, Philo represented Alexandria on a delegation to the emperor Caligula, who wished to be worshipped in the Temple at Jerusalem. He describes this adventure in his *Embassy to Gaius.*

Pliny the Elder (23–79 CE)   Pliny was an enormously learned equestrian from Como in northern Italy, who served in Germany with the future emperor Titus. His huge *Natural History* reflects his wide interests in everything from politics and painting to geography and anthropology. He was the commander of the Roman fleet on the Bay of Naples in 79 CE, when his humanitarianism and his innate curiosity led him to land rescue ships near Pompeii to rescue survivors from the eruption of Vesuvius. He died from inhaling the poisonous fumes.

Plutarch (ca. 50–120s CE)   Plutarch was a wealthy aristocrat from Chaeronea in northern Greece, where he spent most of his life. He wrote many works of philosophy, history, and rhetoric, but he is best known for his *Parallel Lives* of famous Greeks and Romans. He infused these biographies with both research and moral purpose, in the tradition of Greek ethical biography. After placing lives of a famous Greek and a famous Roman beside each other—like Alexander the Great and Julius Caesar—Plutarch wrote a brief comparison with an emphasis on the virtues and vices of the subjects. Plutarch's *Lives* became a classic and since the Renaissance his book has been used for moral instruction.

Seneca (ca. 1–65 CE)   Lucius Seneca, the most renowned Roman philosopher, was born in Córdoba, Spain, into a distinguished family. (His father, who wrote many books on oratory, is known as Seneca the rhetorician.) On the accession of Claudius, the emperor sent Seneca into exile in Corsica, probably for a love affair with Caligula's sister Drusilla. After Claudius married Agrippina—another sister of Caligula—Seneca was recalled to act as tutor to Agrippina's twelve-year-old son, Nero. At Nero's accession five years later in 54 CE, Seneca remained the emperor's closest advisor and a force for moderation. But Nero came to distrust him and he was compelled to commit suicide in 65 CE. Seneca was an advocate of Stoic philosophy, and he wrote many essays and "moral epistles."

Strabo (ca. 64 BCE–21 CE)   Strabo, a Greek born in Asia Minor, was an inveterate traveller who wrote the most important single book of ancient geography. His *Geography* in seventeen books has survived. He boasts of the importance of geography for statesmen, and weaves much historical and philosophical analysis into his book. It was largely written during the reign of Augustus, and Strabo witnessed the effects of the Augustan settlement on the entire Mediterranean.

Suetonius (ca. 70–130 CE)   Gaius Suetonius Tranquillus was a scholar and a pedant more than a historian. He was born to a distinguished family in north Africa, and he rose high in the civil service to the position of chief imperial librarian. He was a member of the intellectual circle around

Trajan, and Pliny called him "most learned." Hadrian dismissed him from his position in 122 CE, perhaps for disrespect shown to the empress Sabina. His *Lives of the Twelve Caesars* is perhaps the most colorful historical source that has survived from the ancient world. Although Suetonius is best known for his scandalous stories, his *Lives* also contain invaluable original sources, such as the private letters of Augustus and Livia, which he found in the imperial archives. The more "sophisticated" historians of the time (like Tacitus) avoided these inelegant documents just as they shunned physical descriptions and personal habits of emperors. Therefore Suetonius' vast, and somewhat undigested, collection of detail is welcome to modern historians.

Tacitus (55–117 CE) Cornelius Tacitus was born into a highly Romanized family in southern Gaul. His own rhetorical brilliance and a fortunate marriage allowed him to advance quickly under the Flavian emperors. Although he withdrew from Rome during the terror of Domitian (93–96 CE), after the emperor's assassination Tacitus returned to political life as consul. He was on friendly terms with the emperors Nerva and Trajan, but his political views were deeply affected by the tyranny of Domitian. His *Annals,* which begins at the death of Augustus, bemoans the loss of free speech and liberty. Although Tacitus might be described as a sentimental republican, he well understood the dangers of civil war and he detested the idea of "mob rule." He understood that there must be emperors, but he wished for, as he calls them, "good emperors." He hoped that the moral and political judgments on the past he expressed so forcefully in his histories would have a positive effect on future generations.

Velleius Paterculus (ca. 20 BCE–ca. 30 CE) Velleius was from an Italian family that had risen to minor prominence during the civil wars. He served as a soldier under Tiberius in Germany and Pannonia, and he became deeply devoted to the imperial family. He entered the Senate and was promoted to the praetorship by Tiberius; his sons reached the consulship under Nero. His brief *Compendium of Roman History* skims the early centuries—the first half of the book goes from the Trojan War to Julius Caesar—before he concentrates on the reigns of Augustus and his hero Tiberius. Although Velleius is not a polished writer, his book provides material that would otherwise be lost as well as the perspective of an "outsider" who truly admires the Julio-Claudian family.

Virgil (70–19 BCE) The greatest of all Roman poets, Publius Vergilius Maro, was born in Mantua in northern Italy. Maecenas subsidized him and brought him into the circle of Augustus. After early poems, which focused on the Italian countryside (*Eclogues; Georgics*), he turned to his great patriotic epic, the *Aeneid.* That account of Aeneas' trek from Troy to Italy to found the Roman people contains many parallels to Augustus and even explicit foreshadowing in the underworld and in the decorations on the shield of Aeneas. For the two thousand years since its first publication, the *Aeneid* has been the most popular work of Latin literature. Through the ages, both pagans and Christians subjected it to their own interpretations, and the medieval poet Dante had Virgil as his master to lead him to the underworld. For others, Virgil was a prophet, even a saint, and Christian meaning was read into his poems. This Augustan poet transcended the politics and values of his own age to speak to eternity.

Vitruvius (d. ca. 20 BCE)   Almost nothing is known of the life of Vitruvius except those few facts scattered through his book *On Architecture*. He was an architect, having designed a basilica, who became a military engineer in Julius Caesar's army. Augustus gave him a pension to enable him to write his book, which is dedicated to the emperor.

Vitruvius believed that an architect required not only a technical education but a wide appreciation of art, philosophy, and literature. His ten books include such topics as sundials, cranes, hydraulics, building materials, and even the choice of site. Because it was the only ancient treatise on architecture that survived, it was enormously important to Renaissance architects.

PART TWO

The Documents

1

The Rise of Octavian

1

AUGUSTUS

The Achievements of Augustus
14 CE

Bronze tablets containing the Res Gestae *(Achievements of Augustus) were set up in front of his tomb and across the empire after the emperor's death as an accounting of his reign. A Greek and Latin text—called the "Queen of Inscriptions"—survives on the wall of a temple to Roma and Augustus in Ankara, Turkey. This provides a magisterial, rose-colored account of his reign, with particular emphasis on the emperor's contributions—military, administrative, and financial—to the Roman people. Constitutional issues are blurred and embarrassing details are ignored. It cloaks Augustus' dominance in traditional republican terminology. It must be read with great caution.*

Augustus begins his Res Gestae *with his emergence in the public arena—his private life mattered not at all. Thus this text differs from his lost* Autobiography, *which covered his youth. Here, as elsewhere, he never mentions the names of his partners, and later rivals, in the triumvirate. His description of the Senate's and people's appointment of him omits the fact that he marched on Rome with a large army to extort the consulship and that the triumvirate was presented to the people as a* fait accompli. *Nevertheless, the* Res Gestae *is invaluable as direct evidence for the way in which Augustus wished to be remembered: as a*

Res Gestae Divi Augusti. Adapted from the translation by Ronald Mellor in *The Historians of Ancient Rome,* ed. Ronald Mellor (New York: Routledge, 1998), 356–64.

generous patron of the state who had restored domestic peace and prosperity after nearly a century of civil conflict.

Shortly after Augustus' death, an appendix was added to the document. Its purpose is uncertain.

Below is a copy of *The Achievements of the Divine Augustus,* by which he brought the entire world under the imperial power of the Roman people, and of the expenses that he incurred for the state and people of Rome; the original text has been inscribed on two bronze pillars set up at Rome.

1. When I was nineteen years old, on my own initiative and at my own expense I raised an army, with which I restored freedom to the state which was oppressed by the power of a clique. For that reason the senate passed honorary decrees enrolling me in its order in the consulship of Gaius Pansa and Aulus Hirtius [43 BCE], granting me the privilege of speaking among the ex-consuls and giving me *imperium*—the right of military command. It ordered me as a **propraetor** together with the consuls to ensure that the state should suffer no harm. In the same year, when both consuls had fallen in battle, the people named me consul and appointed me one of a commission of three *triumvirs* for the re-establishment of the Republic.

2. I drove the murderers of my father into exile and avenged their crime through legal tribunals; and afterwards, when they made war on the Republic, I twice defeated them in battle.[1]

3. I undertook civil and foreign wars by land and sea throughout the whole world, and as victor I spared the lives of all citizens who sought pardon. When foreign nations could safely be pardoned I preferred to preserve rather than to destroy them. Five hundred thousand Roman citizens took a military oath of obedience to me. Of this number, I settled more than three hundred thousand in colonies or sent them back to their hometowns after their service was completed; to all, I gave lands or money as a reward for their military service. I captured six hundred ships, not counting those smaller than **triremes.**

4. Twice I was honored with ovations and I celebrated three triumphs and I was twenty-one times saluted as *imperator.* When the

---

[1]Brutus, Cassius, and other senators assassinated Julius Caesar in 44 BCE; two years later, the triumvirs (Octavian, Marc Antony, and Lepidus) defeated them in the two battles at Philippi.

Senate decreed still more triumphs in my honor, I declined them all. After I had fulfilled the vows I made in each war, I laid the bay leaves from my *fasces* on the Capitol.[2] Fifty-five times the Senate decreed that thanks be offered to the immortal gods on account of successes on land and sea gained by me or by lieutenants acting under my command. The thanksgivings decreed by the Senate occupied 890 days. In my triumphs nine kings or children of kings paraded before my chariot. When I was writing these words, I had been consul thirteen times and was in the thirty-seventh year of tribunician power [14 CE].

5. In the consulship of Marcus Marcellus and Lucius Arruntius [22 BCE], the people and the Senate both offered me the dictatorship, both in my absence and when I was at Rome, but I refused it. During the great famine, I did take charge of the grain supply, which I so administered that, in a few days and at my own expense, I freed the whole city from the fear and present danger of starvation. At that time, the consulship was offered to me, to be held every year for life, but I refused it.

6. In the consulship of Marcus Vinicius and Quintus Lucretius [19 BCE], and afterward in that of Publius and Gnaeus Lentulus [18 BCE], and third in that of Paullus Fabius Maximus and Quintus Tubero [11 BCE], the Senate and the Roman people agreed that I should be appointed sole guardian of laws and morals with supreme power, but I refused any office offered to me that was contrary to the customs of our ancestors. The actions that the Senate wished me to take, I carried out through my tribunician power. On five occasions, at my own request, I received from the Senate a colleague in that office.

7. I was triumvir for the re-establishment of the Republic for ten consecutive years. Up to the day of writing I have been *princeps senatus* for forty years. I am High Priest, *augur,* member of the religious board of fifteen, board of seven for religious feasts, Arval brother, *sodalis Titius,* Fetial priest.[3]

8. In my fifth consulship [29 BCE], I increased the number of **patricians** at the command of the people and the Senate. I revised the roll of the Senate three times. In my sixth consulship [28 BCE] with Marcus Agrippa as colleague, I held a census of the people, and I performed a *lustrum* [purification rites that accompany a census] after a

---

[2] A magistrate's ceremonial axes (*fasces*), the sign of military authority, were festooned with bay leaves.

[3] An *augur* was a priest charged with observing omens, while the Arval brotherhood, the *sodalis Titius,* and the Fetial priesthood were all colleges of priests.

lapse of forty-one years; at that census 4,063,000 Roman citizens were enrolled. Then I performed a second census with consular power and without a colleague, in the consulship of Gaius Censorinus and Gaius Asinius [8 BCE]; in that census 4,233,000 citizens were registered. Third, I performed a census with consular power, with my son Tiberius Caesar as colleague, in the consulship of Sextus Pompeius and Sextus Appuleius [14 CE]; at that census 4,937,000 citizens were registered. By new laws that I proposed, I restored many exemplary practices of our ancestors, which were falling out of use in our own time, and I myself transmitted many exemplars to be imitated by posterity.

9. The Senate decreed that every fifth year the consuls and priests should undertake vows for my health. In fulfillment of these vows games were often celebrated in my lifetime, sometimes by the four most distinguished colleges of priests, sometimes by the consuls. Moreover, all the citizens, individually and on behalf of their towns, have unanimously and continuously offered sacrifices for my health at all the seats of the gods.

10. By decree of the Senate my name was inserted in the hymn of the Salian brotherhood, and it was enacted by law that my person should be forever inviolable and that I should hold the tribunician power as long as I live. When the people offered me the High Priesthood, which my father had held, I refused to replace in that office my colleague who was still alive. Several years later, after the death of the man who had seized it during civil disturbance,[4] I accepted this priesthood, in the consulship of Publius Sulpicius and Gaius Valgius [12 BCE], and such a crowd from all of Italy assembled for my election as was never before recorded at Rome.

11. In honor of my return, the Senate consecrated the altar of *Fortuna Redux* [Fortune Who Brings Back] before the temples of Honor and Virtue at the Porta Capena, and it ordered that the priests and **Vestal virgins** should make a sacrifice there each year on the anniversary of my return to the city from Syria in the consulship of Quintus Lucretius and Marcus Vinicius [19 BCE], and it named the day the Augustalia from my name.

12. At the same time, by decree of the Senate, some of the **praetors** and tribunes of the plebs, with the consul Quintus Lucretius and the leading men, were sent to Campania to meet me, an honor that has been decreed to no one else up to the present day. After I successfully handled affairs in Spain and Gaul and returned to Rome in the consulship of Tiberius Nero and Publius Quintilius [13 BCE], the Sen-

[4]Marcus Lepidus.

ate decreed that an altar of the Augustan Peace (*Ara Pacis Augustae*) should be consecrated in the Campus Martius in honor of my return, at which the magistrates, priests, and Vestal virgins were ordered to make an annual sacrifice.

13. Our ancestors wished that the gateway of Janus Quirinus should be shut whenever victory had secured peace on land and sea throughout the whole empire of the Roman people. From the foundation of the city down to my birth, the tradition is that it was shut only twice, but while I was *princeps* the Senate voted to shut it on three occasions.[5]

14. To honor me, the Senate and Roman people designated my sons Gaius and Lucius Caesar, whom Fortune took from me as young men, as consuls when they were fourteen, providing that they should only enter that magistracy after five years. And the Senate decreed that from the day when they entered into public life they should take part in the councils of state. Furthermore, the whole body of Roman *equites* hailed each one as Leader of the Youth and presented them with silver shields and spears.

15. To the Roman plebs I paid each man 300 sesterces under my father's will, and in my own name I gave them 400 each from the booty of war in my fifth consulship [29 BCE]. In my tenth consulship [24 BCE], I again paid out of my own inheritance a bonus of 400 sesterces to each man, and, in my eleventh consulship [23 BCE], I bought grain with my own money and made twelve food distributions. In the twelfth year of my tribunician power [12 BCE], I gave every man 400 sesterces for the third time. These grants of mine never reached fewer than 250,000 persons. In the eighteenth year of my tribunician power and my twelfth consulship [5 BCE], I gave 240 sesterces apiece to 320,000 members of the urban plebs. In my fifth consulship, I gave 1,000 sesterces out of booty to every one of the colonists drawn from my soldiers; about 120,000 men in colonies received this bonus at the time of my triumph. In my thirteenth consulship [2 BCE], I gave 240 sesterces apiece to the plebs who then received public grain; there were a bit more than 200,000 persons.

16. I paid cash to the towns for the lands that I granted to soldiers in my fourth consulship [30 BCE], and later in the consulship of Marcus Crassus and Gnaeus Lentulus [14 BCE]. I paid a total of about 600,000,000 sesterces for Italian land, and about 260,000,000 sesterces

---

[5]It had been closed under King Numa and after the First Punic War in 235 BCE. Under Augustus it was closed in 29 BCE after the end of the civil war, and in 25 BCE after his war in Spain. The third time is uncertain.

for provincial lands. In the recollection of my contemporaries, I was the first and only one to have done this of all who founded military colonies in Italy or the provinces.[6] Later, in the consulships of Tiberius Nero and Gnaeus Piso, of Gaius Antistius and Decimus Laelius, of Gaius Calvisius and Lucius Pasienus, of Lucius Lentulus and Marcus Messalla and of Lucius Caninius and Quintus Fabricius I paid cash bonuses to soldiers whom I settled in their hometowns after discharge, and for this I spent about 400,000,000 sesterces.

17. Four times I helped the treasury with my own money so that I transferred to the administrators of the treasury 150,000,000 sesterces. In the consulship of Marcus Lepidus and Lucius Arruntius, I paid 170,000,000 sesterces from my inheritance to the military treasury, which was founded by my advice so that cash bonuses could be paid to soldiers who had served for twenty years or more.

18. Beginning in the consulship of Gnaeus and Publius Lentulus [18 BCE], whenever the taxes were inadequate, I distributed from my own funds and my inheritance both grain and money, sometimes to 100,000 persons, sometimes to many more.

19. I built the Senate House and the porch next to it; the temple of Apollo on the Palatine with its porticoes; the temple of the deified Julius; the Lupercal cave; the portico at the Flaminian **circus,** which I permitted to bear the name of the portico of Octavius after the man who erected an earlier portico on the same site; the imperial box at the Circus Maximus; the temples of Jupiter the Subduer and Jupiter the Thunderer on the Capitol; the temple of Quirinus; the temples of Minerva, of Queen Juno, and of Jupiter Libertas on the Aventine Hill; the temple of the *Lares* at the head of the Sacred Way; the temple of the *Di Penates* (household spirits) on the Velian Hill; the temple of Youth; and the temple of the Great Mother on the Palatine Hill.

20. I rebuilt the Capitol and the theater of Pompey—both at great expense—without inscribing my own name. I repaired the channels of the aqueducts, which in several places were collapsing through age, and I doubled the supply of the Marcian aqueduct by bringing in a new spring. I completed the Forum Julium and the basilica between the temples of Castor and Saturn, works begun and almost finished by my father, and when that same basilica was destroyed by fire, I began to rebuild it on an enlarged site, in the name of my sons, and in case I do not finish it in my lifetime, I have ordered my heirs to complete it. In my sixth consulship [28 BCE], I restored eighty-two temples of the

---

[6]Previously generals, including Octavian in 41 BCE, had confiscated land without compensation for their soldiers.

gods in the city on the authority of the senate, neglecting none that needed repair at that time. In my seventh consulship [27 BCE], I rebuilt the Via Flaminia from the city to Rimini, and all the bridges except the Mulvian and the Minucian.

21. I built the temple of Mars the Avenger and the Forum Augustum on my own land from the proceeds of booty. On ground largely bought from private owners, I built a theater next to the temple of Apollo, and called it after my son-in-law Marcus Marcellus. From the booty of war I consecrated dedications on the Capitol and in the temples of the deified Julius, of Apollo, of Vesta, and of Mars the Avenger, which cost me about 100,000,000 sesterces. In my fifth consulship [29 BCE], I gave back 35,000 pounds of gold crowns contributed by the cities and colonies of Italy to my triumphal celebrations, and thereafter, whenever I was saluted as *imperator,* I refused the gold crowns that the cities and colonies continued to vote with the same kindness as before.

22. I presented three gladiatorial games in my own name and five in the name of my sons or grandsons; at these games about 10,000 men fought. Twice in my own name and a third time in that of my grandson I presented to the people spectacles of athletes summoned from all parts. I gave games in my own name four times and, in place of other magistrates, twenty-three times. For the board of fifteen, as its president with Marcus Agrippa as my colleague, I presented the Secular Games in the consulship of Gaius Furnius and Gaius Silanus [17 BCE]. In my thirteenth consulship [2 BCE], I was the first to present the games of Mars, which since that time have been given annually by the consuls by a decree of the Senate. Twenty-six times I presented in my own name or in that of my sons and grandsons beast-hunts with African animals in the circus, forum, or amphitheater, during which about 3,500 beasts were killed.

23. I presented a display of a naval battle as a show for the people across the Tiber in a place now occupied by the grove of the Caesars, where a site 1,800 feet long and 1,200 broad was excavated. In that spot thirty beaked triremes or biremes and more smaller vessels engaged in battle. In these fleets about 3,000 men fought in addition to the rowers.

24. After my victory, I replaced in the temples of all the cities of the province of Asia the ornaments that my former enemy, after looting those temples, had taken for his private use.[7] Some eighty silver statues

---

[7] Even forty-five years after the battle of Actium in 31 BCE, Augustus refused to refer to Marc Antony by name.

of me, standing, mounted, and in four-horse chariots, were set up in Rome; I myself removed them, and with the money from them I placed golden offerings in the temple of Apollo, in my name and in the name of those who had honored me with the statues.

25. I freed the sea of pirates.[8] In that war I captured about 30,000 slaves who had fled from their masters and taken up arms against the state, and I returned them to their masters for punishment. The whole of Italy voluntarily swore an oath of allegiance to me and demanded me to be Leader in the war which I won at Actium. The Gallic and Spanish provinces, Africa, Sicily, and Sardinia swore the same oath. More than 700 senators fought under my standards at that time, including eighty-three who previously or subsequently (down to the day this was written) were made consuls, and about 170 who were appointed priests.

26. I expanded the frontiers of all those provinces of the Roman people bordered by peoples not subject to our government. I brought peace to the Gallic and Spanish provinces as well as to Germany, an area bounded by the ocean from Cadiz to the mouth of the Elbe. I brought peace to the Alps, from the region near the Adriatic all the way to the Tuscan Sea, yet without waging an unjust war on any people. My fleet sailed through the ocean from the mouth of the Rhine eastward to the territory of the Cimbri, a region that no Roman had visited before either by land or sea, and the Cimbri, Charydes, Semnones, and other German peoples of that region sent envoys to seek my friendship and that of the Roman people. At my command and under my auspices two armies were led about the same time into Ethiopia and Arabia Felix; vast enemy forces of both peoples were cut down in battle and many towns were captured. Ethiopia was invaded as far as the town of Nabata, which is next to Meroe; in Arabia the army advanced into the territory of the Sabaeans to the town of Mariba.

27. I added Egypt to the empire of the Roman people.[9] I might have made Greater Armenia a province after its king, Artaxes, was killed, but I preferred, following the precedent of our ancestors, to give that kingdom to Tigranes, son of King Artavasdes and grandson of King Tigranes, acting through Tiberius Nero, who was then my stepson.

---

[8]Augustus refers to his war against Sextus Pompey in 36 BCE.

[9]Although Augustus did conquer Egypt, it remained the personal property of the emperor—the Egyptians regarded him as the Pharaoh—and the province was administered in that way.

When the same people later rebelled and were subdued by my son Gaius, I handed them over to be ruled by King Ariobarzanes, son of Artabazus, king of the Medes, and after his death by his son Artavasdes. When he was murdered, I sent Tigranes, an heir of the royal Armenian house, into that kingdom. I recovered all the provinces east of the Adriatic sea, together with Cyrene, the greater part of them being then occupied by kings.[10] I had earlier recovered Sicily and Sardinia, which had been seized in the slave war.[11]

28. I established colonies of soldiers in Africa, Sicily, Macedonia, both Spanish provinces, Achaea, Asia, Syria, Gallia Narbonensis, and Pisidia. Italy also has twenty-eight colonies founded under my authority, which have become densely populated in my lifetime.

29. By defeating my enemies I recovered in Spain, in Gaul, and from the Dalmatians military standards lost by other commanders. I forced the Parthians to restore to me the spoils and standards of three Roman armies and to beg as suppliants for the friendship of the Roman people.[12] Those standards I placed in the inner shrine of the temple of Mars the Avenger.

30. The Pannonian tribes, which a Roman army had never approached before I was *princeps,* were conquered by Tiberius Nero, who was then my stepson and legate. I added them to the empire of the Roman people, and extended the frontier of Illyricum to the bank of the Danube River. When an army of Dacians crossed to this side of the Danube, it was defeated and routed under my auspices, and later my army crossed the Danube and forced the Dacian peoples to submit to the orders of the Roman people.[13]

31. Embassies were often sent to me from kings in India, which had never been seen by any Roman leader.[14] The Bastarnae, Scythians, and the kings of the Sarmatians who live on both sides of the river Don, and the kings of the Albanians and the Iberians and the Medes sent embassies to seek our friendship.

32. The following kings fled to me as suppliants: Tiridates, king of Parthia, and later Phraates son of King Phraates; Artavasdes, king of

[10]Antony had allowed kings (like Herod of Judaea) to administer Roman provinces.

[11]Another derogatory reference to the war with Sextus Pompey.

[12]Standards lost by Crassus at Carrhae (53 BCE) and Marc Antony in 40 and 36 BCE. They were returned in 20 BCE as a result of a negotiated diplomatic settlement.

[13]It was an exaggeration to regard the Dacians north of the Danube as Roman subjects, but the contemporary Greek geographer Strabo agrees.

[14]Two embassies from India reached Rome in 25 and 20 BCE, and land trade was expanding.

the Medes; Artaxares, king of the Adiabeni; Dumnobellaunus and Tincommius, kings of the Britons; Maelo, king of the Sugambri; and the king of the Marcomanni and Suebi. The king of Parthia, Phraates, son of Orodes, sent all his sons and grandsons to me in Italy, not because he had been overcome in war, but because he sought our friendship by pledging his children. While I was the *princeps,* very many other peoples, who had never previously exchanged embassies or had friendly relations with us, have experienced the good faith of the Roman people.

33. The Parthians and Medians sent to me noble ambassadors who sought and received kings from me, for the Parthians Vonones, son of King Phraates, grandson of King Orodes, and for the Medes, Ariobarzanes, son of King Artavasdes, grandson of King Ariobarzanes.

34. In my sixth and seventh consulships [28–27 BCE], after I had extinguished civil war and, with the consent of all, I was in complete control of the state, I transferred the Republic from my power to the authority of the Senate and Roman people.[15] For this service of mine, I was called Augustus by decree of the Senate, and the doorposts of my house were publicly decorated with bay leaves, a civic crown was fixed over my door, and a golden shield was placed in the Senate House, whose inscription attests that it was given me by the Senate and Roman people because of my courage, clemency, justice, and piety. Thereafter I excelled all in authority, although I possessed no more official power than others who were my colleagues in each office.

35. In my thirteenth consulship [2 BCE], the Senate, the equestrian order, and the entire Roman people called me "Father of the Country," and decreed that this title should be inscribed on the porch of my house, in the Senate House, and in the Forum Augustum below the four-horse chariot, which was placed there in my honor by decree of the Senate. At the time of writing I was in my seventy-sixth year.

Appendix

1 The sum of money that he gave to the treasury or to the Roman plebs or to discharged soldiers was 2,400,000,000 sesterces. 2 He built these new structures: the temples of Mars, of Jupiter the Thunderer and the Subduer, of Apollo, of the deified Julius, of Quirinus, of Minerva, of Queen Juno, of Jupiter Libertas, of the *Lares,* of the *Di Penates,* of the Youth, of the Great Mother; the Lupercal; the imperial

---

[15]Although Augustus referred to the events of 27 BCE as the restoration of the Republic, he in fact retained all effective power.

box at the circus; the Senate House with the porch; the Forum Augustum; the Basilica Julia; the theater of Marcellus; the Octavian portico; the grove of the Caesars beyond the Tiber. 3 He restored the Capitol and sacred buildings to the number of eighty-two, the theater of Pompey, the aqueducts, and the Via Flaminia. 4 The expenditure that he devoted to dramatic shows, to gladiatorial contests, to athletic games and hunts and the sea battle, and the money granted to colonies, cities, towns destroyed by earthquake and fire, or to individual friends and senators to whose property requirement he contributed, are incalculable.

2

NICOLAUS OF DAMASCUS

On Julius Caesar's Admiration for the Young Octavius

20s BCE

Nicolaus' Life of Augustus *covers only the emperor's first nineteen years, down to 44 BCE. When he wrote the book, Nicolaus relied on the emperor's lost* Autobiography *for the private discussions between Julius Caesar and the young Octavius. Nicolaus was a courtier in Rome; his stance toward Augustus is completely uncritical and adulatory.*

After this, Caesar celebrated his triumphs for the Libyan War and the others which he had fought; and he ordered the young Caesar, whom he had now adopted, and who was in a way a son even by nature, on account of the closeness of their relationship, to follow his chariot, having bestowed upon him military decorations, as if he had been his aide in the war. Likewise, at the sacrifices and when entering the temples, he stationed him at his side and he ordered the others to yield precedence to him. Caesar already bore the rank of Imperator, which was the highest according to the Roman usage, and he was

Nicolaus of Damascus, *Life of Augustus* 8; 11. Based on the translation by Clayton Hall (Baltimore: Johns Hopkins University Press, 1923).

highly esteemed in the state. The boy, being his companion both at the theater and at the banquets, and seeing that he conversed kindly with him, as if with his own son, and having by this time become somewhat more courageous, when many of his friends and citizens asked him to intercede for them with Caesar, in matters in which they were in need of aid, looking out for the opportune moment he respectfully asked and was successful; and he became of great value to many of his kinsfolk, for he took care never to ask a favor at an inopportune time, nor when it was annoying to Caesar. And he displayed not a few sparks of kindness and natural intelligence. . . .

Octavius caught up with Caesar in Spain near the city of Calpia. Caesar embraced him as a son and welcomed him, for he had left him at home ill, and he now unexpectedly saw him safe from both enemies and brigands. In fact, he did not let him go from him, but he kept him at his own quarters and mess. He commended his zeal and intelligence, inasmuch as he was the first of those who had set out from Rome to arrive. And he made the point of asking him in conversation, for he was anxious to make a trial of his understanding; and finding that he was sagacious, intelligent, and concise in his replies and that he always answered to the point, his esteem and affection for him increased.

3

SUETONIUS

On the Ides of March:
The Assassination of Julius Caesar
Second Century CE

In this excerpt of Suetonius' Life of Julius Caesar, the biographer provides a dramatic account of Caesar's murder. Marcus Brutus was proud of his descent from Lucius Brutus, who drove the Tarquin kings from Rome in 509 BCE. This left him open to taunts that he did not have the

Suetonius, *Life of Julius Caesar* 80; 82. Based on the translation by J. C. Rolfe, Loeb Classical Library (Cambridge, Mass.: Harvard University Press, 1920).

courage of his ancestor. Despite Caesar's lifelong kindness toward him — perhaps because Caesar had once loved Brutus' mother, Servilia — Brutus became the leader of Caesar's assassins in 44 BCE. Caesar's last words, in Greek, recall their intimacy.

Some wrote on the base of Lucius Brutus' statue, "Oh, that you were still alive"; and on that of Caesar himself:

First of all was Brutus consul, since he drove the kings from Rome;
Since this man drove out the consuls, he at last is made our king.

More than sixty joined the conspiracy against him, led by Gaius Cassius and Marcus and Decimus Brutus. . . . When a meeting of the Senate was called for the Ides of March in the meeting room adjoining the Theater of Gnaeus Pompeius, they readily gave that time and place the preference. . . .

As Caesar took his seat, the conspirators gathered about him as if to pay their respects, and immediately Tillius Cimber, who had assumed the lead, came nearer as though to ask something; and when Caesar with a gesture put him off to another time, Cimber caught his toga by both shoulders; then as Caesar cried, "Why, this is violence!" one of the Cascas stabbed him from one side just below the throat. Caesar caught Casca's arm and ran it through with his stylus, but as he tried to leap to his feet, he was stopped by another wound. When he saw that he was beset on every side by drawn daggers, he muffled his head in his robe, and at the same time drew down its lap to his feet with his left hand, in order to fall more decently, with the lower part of his body also covered. And in this way he was stabbed with twenty-three wounds, uttering not a word, but merely a groan at the first stroke, though some have written that when Marcus Brutus rushed at him, he said in Greek, "You too, my child?"

4

APPIAN

On Octavian's First Confrontation with Antony

Second Century CE

The Greek historian Appian wrote his Civil Wars *two centuries after the events, but it is still the most detailed account of the decade after Caesar's death. When Octavian arrived in Rome after the death of Caesar in the spring of 44 BCE, he found that Marc Antony had taken control of Caesar's war chest and his papers. Octavian argued that as Caesar's heir, he needed the money that Caesar had accumulated for a Parthian War, to distribute the legacies that Caesar had left to the Roman people. Although only eighteen years old, Octavian put Antony on the defensive by suggesting that he had "sold out" to the murderers and the Senate. This was their first confrontation in a struggle that continued until Antony's death in 30 BCE.*

"For the future, Antony, I beg you by the gods who preside over friendship, and by Caesar himself, to change the measures that have been adopted, for you can change them if you wish to; if not, that you will hereafter aid and cooperate with me in punishing the murderers, with the help of the people and of those who are still my father's faithful friends. If you still have regard for the conspirators and the Senate, do not be hard on us. So much for that. You know about my private affairs and the expense I must incur for the legacy which my father directed to be given to the people, and the need for haste lest I seem stingy if I delay, and lest those who have been assigned to colonies be compelled to remain in the city and waste their time on my account. As far as Caesar's property, it was brought immediately after the murder from his house to yours as a safer place. I beg you to take souvenirs, ornaments, and whatever you like to retain from us. But in order that I may pay the legacy to the people, please give me the gold coin that Caesar had collected for his intended wars. That will suffice

---

Appian, *Civil Wars* 3, 17–19. Based on the translation by H. White, Loeb Classical Library (Cambridge, Mass.: Harvard University Press, 1913).

for the distribution to 300,000 men now. For the rest of my expenses I may perhaps borrow from you, if I may be so bold, or from the public treasury on your security, if you will give it, and I will offer my own property for sale at once."

While Octavius was speaking in this fashion Antony was astonished at his freedom of speech and his boldness, which seemed much beyond the bounds of propriety and of his years. He was offended by the words because they were wanting in the respect due to him, and still more by the demand for money, and so he replied severely as follows: "Young man, if Caesar left you the government, together with the inheritance and his name, it is proper for you to ask and for me to give the reasons for my public acts. But the Roman people never surrendered the government to anybody to dispose of in succession, not even when they had kings, whom they expelled and swore never to have any more. This was the very charge that the murderers brought against your father, saying that they killed him because he was no longer leading but reigning. So there is no need of my answering you as to my public acts. For the same reason I release you from any indebtedness to me in the way of gratitude for those acts. They were performed not as a favor to you, but to the people, except in one particular, which was of the greatest importance to Caesar and to yourself. For if, to secure my own safety and to shield myself from enmity, I had allowed honors to be voted to the murderers as tyrannicides, Caesar would have been declared a tyrant, to whom neither glory, nor any kind of honor, nor confirmation of his acts would have been possible; who could make no valid will, have no son, nor any burial of his body, even as a private citizen. The laws provide that the bodies of tyrants shall be cast out unburied, their memory stigmatized, and their property confiscated.

"Understanding these consequences, I struggled for Caesar, for his immortal honor, and his public funeral, not without danger, not without incurring hatred to myself, contending against hot-headed, bloodthirsty men, who, as you know, had already conspired to kill me; and against the Senate, which was displeased with your father on account of his usurped authority. But I willingly chose to incur these dangers and to suffer anything rather than allow Caesar to remain unburied and dishonored—the most valiant man of his time, the most fortunate in every respect, and the one to whom the highest honors were due from me. It is by reason of the dangers I incurred that you enjoy your present distinction as the successor of Caesar, his family, his name, his dignity, his wealth. It was more becoming in you to testify your gratitude to me for these things than to reproach me for concessions made to soothe the Senate. . . ."

5

MARCUS TULLIUS CICERO

Letters Revealing His Views of Young Octavian
44 BCE

In the aftermath of Caesar's assassination, the mood of the conservative statesman Cicero swung from pessimism to optimism and back again. Because he supported the assassins, he at first distrusted young Octavian, while at the same time hoping he could be turned against Antony. He writes to his closest friend, the banker Atticus, as well as to the conspirator Marcus Brutus. Cicero's vanity, which was his greatest weakness as a politician, is clearly evident in these letters in the months after Caesar's murder.

Octavian was well aware that the Ciceronian faction only desired, as one jibe said, "that the young man must be complimented, honored, and—got rid of." They soon learned to their cost that he was shrewder than they had expected. After Octavian defeated Antony in April of 43 BCE, the senators, against Cicero's advice, tried to discard the young man. In fact, he discarded them. He turned back to Antony and, together with Lepidus, they soon proscribed their political enemies. By December, Cicero had been executed.

To Atticus (April 22, 44 BCE)

Ah, my dear Atticus, I fear the Ides of March have brought us nothing beyond exultation, and the satisfaction of our anger and resentment. What news reaches me from Rome! . . . Octavius here treats me with great respect and friendliness. His own people addressed him as "Cae-

Cicero, *Letters to Atticus* 14, 12; *Letters to Brutus* 1, 3; *Letters to Atticus* 16, 8. Adapted from the translation by Evelyn Shuckburgh (London: G. Bell and Sons, 1909–1914).

sar," but Philippus did not, so I did not do so either. I declare that it is impossible for him to be a good citizen. He is surrounded by a number of people, who even threaten our friends with death. He says the present state of things is unendurable. But what do you think of it, when a boy like that goes to Rome, where our liberators cannot be in safety. They indeed will always be illustrious, and even happy, from the consciousness of their great deed. But for us, unless I am mistaken, we shall be ruined. . . .

To Marcus Brutus at Dyrrachium (April 21, 44 BCE)

Our cause seems in a better position: for I feel sure that you have had letters telling you what has happened. The consuls have shown themselves to be the sort of men I have often described them in my letters. In the youthful Caesar indeed there is a surprising natural strain of virtue. Pray heaven we may control him in the flush of honors and popularity as easily as we have held him up to this time. That is certainly a more difficult thing, but nevertheless I trust we can. For the young man has been convinced, and chiefly by my arguments, that our safety is his responsibility, and that at least, if he had not diverted Antony from the city, all would have been lost. Three or four days indeed before this glorious news, the city, struck by a sudden panic, was for pouring out with wives and children to seek you. The same city on the 20th of April, with its fears all dispelled, would rather that you came here than go to you. On that day in very truth I reaped the most abundant harvest of my great labors and my many sleepless nights—that is, at least, if there is a harvest in genuine and well-grounded glory. For I was surrounded by as big a crowd as our city can contain, by whom I was escorted to the Capitol and placed upon the rostra amidst the loudest cheers and applause. I have no vanity in me—and indeed I ought to have none: yet after all everyone's affection, thanks, and congratulations do move my heart, because it is a thing to be proud of that in the hour of the people's salvation I should be the people's hero . . .

To Atticus (November 2, 44 BCE)

When I know what day I am coming to town I will let you know. I must expect some hindrances, and there is illness among my household. On the evening of the 1st I got a letter from Octavian. He is entering upon a serious undertaking. He has won over to his views all the veterans at Casilinum and Calatia. And no wonder: he gives a bounty of 500 **denarii** apiece. Clearly, his view is a war with Antony under his leadership. So I perceive that before many days are over we shall be in arms. But whom are we to follow? Consider his name, consider his age! Again, to begin with, he demands a secret interview with me, at Capua of all places! It is really quite childish if he supposes that it can be kept private. I have written to explain to him that it is neither necessary nor practicable. He sent a certain Caecina of Volterra to me, an intimate friend of his own, who brought me the news that Antony was on his way towards the city with the legion Alauda, was demanding a financial contribution from the towns, and was marching at the head of the legion with colors flying. Octavian wanted my opinion whether he should start for Rome with his army of 3,000 veterans, or should hold Capua, and so intercept Antony's advance, or should join the three Macedonian legions now sailing across the Adriatic, which he hopes are loyal to him. They refused to accept a bonus offered them by Antony, as my informant at least says. They even used grossly insulting language to him, and moved off when he attempted to address them. In short, Octavian offers himself as our military leader, and thinks that our right policy is to stand by him. On my part I advised his making for Rome. For I think that he will have not only the city mob, but, if he can impress them with confidence, the loyalists also on his side. Oh, Brutus, where are you? What an opportunity you are losing? For my part, I did not foresee this, but I thought that something of the sort would happen. Now, I desire to have your advice. Shall I come to Rome or stay on here? Or am I to fly to Arpinum? There is a sense of security about that place! My opinion is—Rome, lest my absence should be remarked, if people think that a blow has been struck. Unravel this difficulty. I was never in greater perplexity.

6

APPIAN

On the Second Triumvirate

Second Century CE

In 43 BCE, the Senate sent the consuls, along with Octavian, to oppose Antony at Mutina in northern Italy. When the consuls died in battle and Antony fled across the Alps, Octavian asked to be welcomed into Rome with a triumphal procession, but he was rebuffed. Understanding that the Senate was merely using him against Antony, Octavian marched on Rome with eight legions and made himself consul. In November 43 BCE, he returned to Mutina and formed a triumvirate with Antony and Lepidus. In this excerpt from his Civil Wars, *the Greek historian Appian recounts how the triumvirs negotiated the future of the Roman world.*

The triumvirs made up a list of those to be condemned to death in the proscriptions of 43 BCE—not only political opponents but private enemies as well. It began as a small list—first seventeen men, then 130 more, then 150 more, and so on. Their heads were returned to the triumvirs for the payment of a bounty and then displayed in the Forum as a warning to all.

We see here the elements of a modern police state: informers with secret identities and slaves paid to betray masters—the decree denouncing Caesar's assassins was little more than an elaborate justification of mass murder.

Octavian and Antony composed their differences on a small, depressed islet in the river Lavinius, near the city of Mutina. Each had five legions of soldiers whom they stationed opposite each other, after which each proceeded with three hundred men to the bridges over the river. Lepidus by himself went before them, searched the island, and waved his military cloak as a signal to them to come. Then each left his three hundred in charge of friends on the bridges and advanced to the middle of the island in plain sight, and there the three sat together in

---

Appian, *Civil Wars* 4, 2; 4, 8–11. Based on the translation of H. White, Loeb Classical Library (Cambridge, Mass.: Harvard University Press, 1913).

council, Octavian in the centre because he was consul. They were in conference from morning till night for two days, and came to these decisions: that Octavian should resign the consulship and that Ventidius should take it for the remainder of the year; that a new magistracy for quieting the civil dissensions should be created by law, which Lepidus, Antony, and Octavian should hold for five years with consular power (for this name seemed preferable to that of dictator, perhaps because of Antony's decree abolishing the dictatorship); that these three should at once designate the yearly magistrates of the city for the five years; that a distribution of the provinces should be made, giving to Antony the whole of Gaul except the part bordering the Pyrenees Mountains, which was called Old Gaul; this, together with Spain, was assigned to Lepidus; while Octavian was to have Africa, Sardinia, and Sicily, and the other islands nearby. . . .

The proscription was in the following words, "Marcus Lepidus, Marcus Antony, and Octavius Caesar, chosen by the people to set in order and regulate the Republic, do declare that, had not perfidious traitors begged for mercy and when they obtained it become the enemies of their benefactors and conspired against them, neither would Julius Caesar have been slain by those whom he saved by his clemency after capturing them in war, whom he admitted to his friendship and upon whom he heaped offices, honors, and gifts; nor should we have been compelled to use this widespread severity against those who have insulted us and declared us public enemies. So, seeing that the malice of those who have conspired against us and by whose hands Gaius Caesar suffered, cannot be mollified by kindness, we prefer to anticipate our enemies rather than suffer at their hands. Let no one who sees what both Caesar and ourselves have suffered consider our action unjust, cruel, or immoderate. Although Caesar was clothed with supreme power, although he was high priest, although he had overthrown and added to our sway the nations most formidable to the Romans, although he was the first man to attempt the untried sea beyond the pillars of Hercules [straits of Gibraltar] and was the discoverer of a country hitherto unknown to the Romans, this man was slain in the midst of the Senate-house, which is designated as sacred, under the eyes of the gods, with twenty-three dastardly wounds, by men whom he had taken prisoners in war and had spared, while some of them he had named as co-heirs of his wealth. After this execrable crime, instead of arresting the guilty wretches, the rest sent them forth as commanders and governors, in which capacity they seized upon the public money, with which they are collecting an army against us and are seeking reinforcements from barbarians ever hostile to Roman rule. Cities subject to Rome that would not obey them they have burned, or ravaged, or leveled to the ground; other cities they have forced by terror to bear arms against the country and against us.

"Some of them we have punished already; and by the aid of divine providence you shall presently see the rest punished. Although the chief part of this work has been finished by us or is well under control, namely the settlement of Spain and Gaul as well as matters here in Italy, one task still remains, and that is to march against Caesar's assassins beyond the sea. On the eve of undertaking this foreign war for you, we do not consider it safe, either for you or for us, to leave other enemies behind to take advantage of our absence and watch for opportunities during the war; nor again do we think that there should be delay on their account, but that we ought rather to sweep them out of our pathway, once for all, seeing that they began the war against us when they voted us and the armies under us public enemies.

"What vast numbers of citizens have they doomed to destruction with us, disregarding the vengeance of the gods and the contempt of mankind! We shall not deal harshly with any multitude of men, nor shall we count as enemies all who opposed us or plotted against us, or those notable for their wealth or their high position; nor shall we kill as many as another man [Sulla] who held the supreme power before us, when he, too, was regulating the commonwealth in civil convulsions, and whom you named the Fortunate on account of his success, even though three persons will have more enemies than one. We shall take vengeance only on the worst and most guilty. This we shall do for your interest no less than for our own, for while we keep up our conflicts you will all be involved necessarily in great dangers, and it is necessary for us also to do something to quiet the army, which has been insulted, irritated, and decreed a public enemy by our common foes. Although we might arrest on the spot whomsoever we had determined on, we prefer to proscribe rather than seize them unawares; and this, too, on your account, so that it may not be in the power of enraged soldiers to exceed their orders against persons not responsible, but that they may be restricted to a certain number designated by name, and spare the others according to order.

"So be it then! Let no one harbor any one of those whose names are hereto appended, or conceal them, or send them away, or be corrupted by their money. Whoever shall be detected in saving, or aiding, or conniving with them we will put on the list of the proscribed without allowing any excuse or pardon. Let those who kill the proscribed bring us their heads and receive the following rewards: to a free man 25,000 Attic drachmas per head; to a slave his freedom and 10,000 Attic drachmas and his master's right of citizenship. Informers shall receive the same rewards. In order that they may remain unknown the names of those who receive the rewards shall not be inscribed in our registers." Such was the language of the proscription of the triumvirate as nearly as it can be rendered from Latin into Greek.

7

TACITUS

A Senatorial View of the Civil War
Second Century CE

Because the historian and senator Tacitus lived during the despotic reigns of Nero and Domitian, he looked back and saw in the beginnings of the principate the seeds of tyranny. As a sentimental republican, he yearned for the time when the Senate had ruled Rome. When he looked back on the civil wars after Caesar's death, he believed that the brave had died; only the cowards were left. We might find Tacitus' disavowal of "bitterness and partiality" rather naïve, but he means that because Augustus and Tiberius had neither harmed nor rewarded him, he had no conflict of interest. Still, his political stance against Augustus is clear.

Rome at the beginning was ruled by kings. Freedom and the consulship were established by Lucius Brutus. Dictatorships were held for a temporary crisis. The power of the decemvirs did not last beyond two years, nor was the consular jurisdiction of the military tribunes of long duration.[16] The despotisms of Cinna and Sulla were brief; the rule

---

[16]The decemvirs were a commission of ten appointed in 451 BCE to create a written law code, while military tribunes held the power of consuls between 444 and 367 BCE.

Tacitus, *Annals* 1, 1–2. Based on the translation of A. J. Church and W. J. Brodribb (London: Macmillan, 1886).

of Pompey and of Crassus soon gave way to Caesar; the armies of Lepidus and Antony to Augustus, who, when the world was wearied by civil strife, brought it under his power [*imperium*] with the title of "Prince." But the successes and reverses of the old Roman people have been recorded by famous historians, and fine intellects were available to describe the times of Augustus, till growing sycophancy scared them away. The histories of Tiberius, Gaius Caligula, Claudius, and Nero, while they were in power, were falsified through terror, and after their deaths were written under the anger of a recent hatred. Hence my purpose is to relate a few facts about Augustus — especially his last actions, then the reign of Tiberius, and all which follows, without either bitterness or partiality, which I in no way share.

When, after the destruction of Brutus and Cassius, there was no longer any army of the Commonwealth, when Pompey was crushed in Sicily, and when, with Lepidus pushed aside and Antony slain, even the Julian faction had only Octavian left to lead it, then, dropping the title of triumvir, and giving out that he was a consul, and was satisfied with a tribune's authority for the protection of the people,[17] Augustus seduced the soldiers with bonuses, the people with food, and everyone with the sweetness of peace. Thus he gradually grew stronger, as he concentrated in himself the functions of the Senate, the magistrates, and the laws. He was wholly unopposed, for the boldest spirits had fallen in battle, or in the proscriptions, while the remaining nobles, so eager to be slaves, were raised higher by wealth and promotion, so that, benefiting from the revolution, they preferred the safety of the present to the dangerous past. Nor did the provinces dislike that situation, for they distrusted the government of the Senate and the people, because of the rivalries between the leading men and the rapacity of the officials, while the protection of the laws was unavailing, as they were continually undermined by violence, intrigue, and finally by corruption.

[17]During the Roman Republic the tribunes were regarded as the protectors of the common people. Augustus gave himself the "tribune's authority" to propose and veto legislation in the interests of the people.

8

PLUTARCH

On Cleopatra's Seduction of Mark Antony

Second Century CE

This famous description of the meeting of Antony and Cleopatra at Tar-
sus (on the coast of modern Turkey) in 41 BCE forms the basis of Shake-
speare's play and numerous paintings. The Greek biographer Plutarch,
in his Life of Antony, *attributes Cleopatra's fascination to her character,*
voice, and intelligence rather than merely to her physical beauty. Antony
knew Cleopatra as Julius Caesar's lover, but in the intervening years she
had provided funds to Brutus and Cassius. Antony had serious business
with her, but she obviously thought it best to persuade him to put pleasure
before business.

She received several letters, both from Antony and from his friends, to
summon her, but she took no account of these orders; and at last, as if
in mockery of them, she came sailing up the river Cydnus, in a barge
with gilded stern and outspread sails of purple, while oars of silver
beat time to the music of flutes and fifes and harps. She herself lay all
alone under a canopy of cloth of gold, dressed as Venus in a picture,
and beautiful young boys, like painted Cupids, stood on each side to
fan her. Her maids were dressed like sea nymphs and graces, some
steering at the rudder, some working at the ropes. The perfumes dif-
fused themselves from the vessel to the shore, which was covered
with crowds, some following the ship up the river on either bank, others running out of the city to see the sight. The marketplace was quite
emptied, and Antony at last was left alone sitting upon the platform;
while the word spread among the crowd that Venus was come to feast
with Bacchus, for the common good of Asia. On her arrival, Antony
sent her an invitation to come to supper. She thought it more suitable
that he should come to her; so, willing to show his good humor and

---

Plutarch, *Life of Antony* 26–27. Based on John Dryden's translation as revised by A. H.
Clough (Boston: Little, Brown, 1863).

courtesy, he complied and went. He found the preparations to receive him magnificent beyond expression, but nothing was so admirable as the great number of lights. A large number of branches with lights in them suddenly were lowered, some in squares, and others in circles, that the whole thing was a spectacle that has seldom been equaled for beauty.

The next day Antony invited her to supper, and wanted to outdo her in lavishness as well as in ingenuity. But he found he was beaten in both, and was so well convinced of it that he was himself the first to make fun of his own lack of imagination and his rustic awkwardness. When she realized that his sense of humor was broad and crude, more like a soldier than a courtier, she quickly responded the same way, without any sort of reluctance or reserve. For her actual beauty, it is said, was not in itself so remarkable that none could be compared with her, or that no one could see her without being struck by it, but the force of her presence was irresistible. Her physical attraction, together with the charm of her conversation, and the character in everything she said or did, was something bewitching. It was a pleasure merely to hear the sound of her voice, with which, like an instrument of many strings, she could pass from one language to another; so that there were few barbarian nations for whom she used an interpreter; to most of them she spoke herself, as to the Ethiopians, Troglodytes, Hebrews, Arabians, Syrians, Medes, Parthians, and many others, whose language she had learned. It was all the more surprising because most of her predecessors barely bothered to learn Egyptian, and several of them quite abandoned the Macedonian language.

9

CASSIUS DIO

On Octavian's Propaganda against Antony
Third Century CE

Stories of Antony's shameful submission to Cleopatra are numerous in the later sources. The Greek historian Cassius Dio included these anecdotes in his general Roman History, *which remains our most detailed source for the time of Augustus. These slanders were presumably widely circulated as part of Octavian's propaganda campaign against the lovers — both before and after their deaths.*

For Cleopatra had enslaved Antony so absolutely that she persuaded him to act as sponsor of the gymnasium to the Alexandrians. She was called "queen" and "mistress" by him, had Roman soldiers in her bodyguard, and all of these inscribed her name upon their shields. She used to frequent the marketplace with him, joined him in the management of festivals and in the hearing of lawsuits, and rode with him even in the cities, or else was carried in a chair while Antony accompanied her on foot along with her eunuchs. He also termed his headquarters "the palace," sometimes wore an oriental dagger at his belt, dressed in a manner not in accordance with the customs of his native land, and let himself be seen even in public upon a gilded couch or a chair of that kind. He posed with her for portrait paintings and statues, he representing Osiris or Dionysus and she Selene or Isis. This more than all else made him seem to have been bewitched by her through some enchantment. For she so charmed and enthralled not only him but also the rest who had any influence with him that she conceived the hope of ruling even the Romans; and whenever she used an oath her strongest phrase in swearing was by her purpose to dispense justice on the Capitol.

Cassius Dio, *Roman History* 50, 5. Based on the translation of Earnest Cary, Loeb Classical Library (Cambridge, Mass.: Harvard University Press, 1917).

10

SUETONIUS

On Antony's Propaganda against Octavian in 34 BCE

Second Century CE

The ancient sources contain a great deal of scurrilous material on Antony (and Cleopatra) because Octavian was the victor, and the victors write history. The biographer Suetonius also records in his Life of Augustus *some stories that show that Antony and his supporters were responding in kind with slanders against Octavian.*

Not even his friends denied that Octavian was given to adultery, although they excused it as committed not from passion but from politics, so he could more easily keep track of his enemies' plans through the women of their households. Mark Antony charged him, besides his hasty marriage with Livia, with taking the wife of an ex-consul from her husband's dining room before his very eyes into a bedroom, and bringing her back to the table with her hair in disorder and her ears glowing; that Scribonia was divorced because she openly expressed her jealousy at a rival; and that his friends acted as his pimps, and stripped and inspected matrons and well-grown girls, as if Toranius the slave-dealer were putting them up for sale. Antony also writes to Augustus himself in the following familiar terms, when he had not yet wholly broken with him privately or publicly:

> What has made such a change in you? Because I sleep with the queen? She is my wife. Am I just beginning this, or was it nine years ago? What then of you — do you sleep only with Livia? Good luck to you if when you read this letter you have not slept with Tertulla or Terentilla or Rufilla or Salvia Titisenia, or all of them. Does it matter where or with whom you take your pleasure?

Suetonius, *Life of Augustus* 69. Based on the translation of J. C. Rolfe, Loeb Classical Library (Cambridge, Mass.: Harvard University Press, 1920).

11

CASSIUS DIO

On the Conquest of Egypt
Third Century CE

The story of Cleopatra's meeting with Octavian soon after Antony's death in 30 BCE appears in Plutarch's Parallel Lives *and Cassius Dio's* Roman History, *but both versions must go back to Octavian himself, for he was the only survivor of the conversations. (They would have been in Greek, which both spoke.) We can understand why he would like to boast of her attempted seduction, and likewise take credit for his refusal of her. But did it happen? It seems plausible that Cleopatra would have tried, but her "speeches" should be taken with a large grain of salt.*

Cleopatra accordingly prepared a splendid apartment and a costly couch, and moreover arrayed herself with affected negligence—indeed, her mourning garb wonderfully became her—and seated herself upon the couch. She placed beside her many varied images of his father Julius, and in her bosom she put all the letters that his father had sent her. When, after this, Octavian entered, she leaped gracefully to her feet and cried: "Hail, master—for Heaven has granted you the mastery and taken it from me. But surely you can see with your own eyes how your father looked when he visited me on many occasions, and you have heard people tell how he honored me in various ways and made me queen of the Egyptians. That you may, however, learn something about me from him himself, take and read the letters which he wrote me with his own hand."

After she had spoken thus, she proceeded to read many passionate expressions of Julius Caesar. And now she would lament and kiss the letters, and again she would fall before his images and do them reverence. She kept turning her eyes toward Octavian and bewailing her fate in musical accents. She spoke in melting tones, saying at one time, "Of what use are these letters to me, Caesar?" And to anyone

---

Cassius Dio, *Roman History* 51, 12–13; 17; 21. Based on the translation of Earnest Cary, Loeb Classical Library (Cambridge, Mass.: Harvard University Press, 1917).

nearby, "But in this man here thou also art alive for me"; again, "Would that I had died before you," and still again, "But if I have him, I have you."

Such were the subtleties of speech and of attitude which she employed, and sweet were the glances she cast at him and the words she murmured to him. Now Octavian was not insensible to the ardor of her speech and the appeal to his passions, but he pretended to be; and letting his eyes rest upon the ground, he merely said: "Be of good cheer, woman, and keep a stout heart; for you shall suffer no harm." She was greatly distressed because he would neither look at her nor say anything about the kingdom nor even utter a word of love, and falling at his knees, she said with an outburst of sobbing: "I neither wish to live nor can I live, Caesar. But I beg this favor of you in memory of your father, that, since Heaven gave me to Antony after him, I may also die with Antony. Would that I had perished then, straightway after Julius! But since it was decreed by fate that I should suffer this affliction also, send me to Antony; grudge me not burial with him, in order that, as it is because of him I die, so I may dwell with him even in Hades."

Such words she uttered, expecting to move him to pity, but Caesar made no answer to them; fearing, however, that she might destroy herself, he exhorted her again to be of good cheer, and not only did not remove any of her attendants but also took special care of her, that she might add brilliance to his triumph. This purpose she suspected, and regarding that fate as worse than a thousand deaths, she conceived a genuine desire to die, and not only addressed many entreaties to Caesar that she might perish in some manner or other, but also devised many plans herself. But when she could accomplish nothing, she feigned a change of heart, pretending to set great hopes in him and also in Livia. She said she would sail of her own free will, and she made ready some treasured articles of adornment to use as gifts, in the hope that by these means she might inspire belief that it was not her purpose to die, and so might be less closely guarded and thus be able to destroy herself. And so it came about. For as soon as the others and Epaphroditus, who was guarding her, had come to believe that she really felt as she pretended, and neglected to keep a careful watch, she made her preparations to die as painlessly as possible. First she gave a sealed message, in which she begged Caesar to order that she be buried beside Antony, to Epaphroditus himself to deliver, pretending that it contained some other matter, and then, having by this excuse freed herself of his presence, she set about her task. She put on her most beautiful apparel, arranged her body in most seemly fashion, took in her hands all the emblems of royalty, and so died. . . .

[Dio makes it clear in this passage that Octavian intended to treat Egypt differently from the other Roman provinces, as the personal possession of the emperor. There was clearly significant resistance to Roman rule — not least in the strange natural phenomena that were seen as divine omens. But most important, we see the economic results of the conquest of Egypt.]

Afterwards he made Egypt tributary and gave it in charge of Cornelius Gallus. For in view of the populousness of both the cities and the country, the unpredictable character of the inhabitants, and the extent of the grain supply and of the wealth, so far from daring to entrust the land to any senator, he would not even grant a senator permission to live in it, except as he personally made the concession to him by name. On the other hand, he did not allow the Egyptians to be senators in Rome; but whereas he made various grants to the several other cities, he commanded the Alexandrians to conduct their government without senators since, I suppose, he feared their capacity for revolution. . . .

So much for these events. In the palace quantities of treasure were found. For Cleopatra had taken practically all the offerings from even the holiest shrines and so helped the Romans swell their spoils without incurring any defilement on their own part. Large sums were also obtained from every man against whom any accusation was brought. And apart from these, all the rest, even though no particular complaint could be lodged against them, had two-thirds of their property demanded of them. Out of this wealth all the troops received what was promised to them, and those who were with Octavian at the time got in addition a thousand sesterces on condition of not plundering the city. Repayment was made in full to those who had previously advanced loans, and to both the senators and the *equites* who had taken part in the war large sums were given. Finally, the Roman Empire was enriched and its temples adorned.

[The celebration of the triple triumph brought large distributions of cash to the soldiers and the people. It is rare to find a precise economic statement in an ancient source, but Cassius Dio here tells us that the abundance of cash lowered the interest rate from 12 percent to 4 percent. The cash awards of 29 BCE had an enormous effect on the economy.]

In the course of the summer Octavian Caesar crossed over to Greece and to Italy; and when he entered the city, not only all the citizens offered sacrifice, as has been mentioned, but even the consul Valerius Potitus. Caesar, to be sure, was consul all that year as for the two preceding years, but Potitus was the successor of Sextus. It was he who publicly and in person offered sacrifices on behalf of the Senate and of the people upon Caesar's arrival, a thing that had never been done in the case of any other person. After this Caesar bestowed eulogies and honors upon his lieutenants, as was customary, and to Agrippa he further granted, among other distinctions, a dark blue flag in honor of his naval victory, and he gave gifts to the soldiers. To the people he distributed four hundred sesterces apiece, first to the men who were adults, and afterwards to the children because of his nephew Marcellus. In view of all this, and because he would not accept from the cities of Italy the gold required for the crowns they had voted him, and because, furthermore, he not only paid all the debts he himself owed to others, but also did not insist on the payment of others' debts to him, the Romans forgot all their unpleasant experiences and viewed his triumph with pleasure, quite as if the vanquished had all been foreigners.

So vast an amount of money, in fact, circulated through all parts of the city alike, that the price of goods rose and loans for which the borrower had been glad to pay twelve percent could now be had for one third that rate. As for the triumph, Caesar celebrated on the first day his victories over the Pannonians and Dalmatians, the Iapydes and their neighbours, and some Germans and Gauls. . . . On the second day the naval victory at Actium was commemorated, and on the third the subjugation of Egypt. Now all the processions proved notable, thanks to the spoils from Egypt—in such quantities, indeed, had spoils been gathered there that they sufficed for all the processions—but the Egyptian celebration surpassed them all in costliness and magnificence. Among other features, an effigy of the dead Cleopatra upon a couch was carried by, so that in a way she, too, together with the other captives and with her children, Alexander, also called Helios, and Cleopatra, called also Selene, was a part of the spectacle and a trophy in the procession. After this came Caesar, riding into the city behind them all. He did everything in the customary manner, except that he permitted his fellow-consul and the other magistrates, contrary to precedent, to follow him along with the senators who had participated in the victory; for it was usual for such officials to march in advance and for only the senators to follow.

2

Augustus as *Princeps*

12

SUETONIUS

On the Restoration of the Republic
Second Century CE

In his biography of Augustus, Suetonius gives the image of Augustus as holding power only reluctantly after 27 BCE—the same image that appears in his own Res Gestae. *Of course, Augustus knew that a return to the "Republic" would bring renewed civil war.*

He twice thought of restoring the Republic; first immediately after the overthrow of Antony, remembering that his rival had often made the charge that it was his fault that it was not restored; and again in the weariness of a lingering illness [23 BCE], when he went so far as to summon the magistrates and the Senate to his house, and submit an account of the general condition of the Empire. Realizing, however, that as he himself would not be free from danger if he should retire, and it would also be dangerous to trust the State to the control of more than one man, he continued to keep it in his hands. It is not easy to say whether his intentions or their results were the better. His good intentions he not only expressed from time to time but put on record as well in an edict in the following words: "May it be my privilege to establish the State in a firm and secure position, and reap from that act the fruit that I desire; but only if I may be called the author of the

Suetonius, *Life of Augustus* 28. Based on the translation by J. C. Rolfe, Loeb Classical Library (Cambridge, Mass.: Harvard University Press, 1920).

best possible government, and bear with me the hope when I die that the foundations which I have laid for the State will remain unshaken."

13

CASSIUS DIO

On the Illness of Augustus in 23 BCE
Third Century CE

Cassius Dio's history also records Augustus' brush with death in 23 BCE, but he makes no mention of any restoration of the Republic. Augustus may have been testing the reaction to his naming a successor and may have decided to leave power with Agrippa without making a formal transfer.

When Augustus was consul for the eleventh time, with Calpurnius Piso, he again fell so ill that there seemed no hope of recovery. At any rate, he arranged everything as if he were about to die, and gathered about him the magistrates and the foremost senators and *equites*. He did not, to be sure, appoint a successor, although all were expecting that Marcellus would be chosen for this position. After talking with the senators for awhile about the public affairs, he gave Piso the list of the armies and of the public revenues written in a book, and handed his ring to Agrippa. And although he lost the power of attending even to the most urgent matters, yet a certain Antonius Musa restored him to health by means of cold baths and cold potions. For this, Musa received a great deal of money from both Augustus and the Senate, as well as the right to wear gold rings (for he was a freedman). He was also granted exemption from taxes, both for himself and for all other doctors, not only those living at the time but also those of future generations.

Cassius Dio, *Roman History* 53, 30. Based on the translation of Earnest Cary, Loeb Classical Library (Cambridge, Mass.: Harvard University Press, 1917).

14

SUETONIUS

Some Anecdotes and Descriptions concerning Augustus

Second Century CE

Suetonius here collects anecdotes to demonstrate the affability, modesty, and general humanity of Augustus. Here again, the source was probably Augustus' own writings or a court historian.

As a biographer, Suetonius always includes in his Lives *the sort of physical description that a Roman writer of history would regard as vulgar and tasteless. Yet this sort of material is likely to be more reliable than the subjective judgments about the political intentions of the emperors and their families that we find in Tacitus.*

He always shrank from the title of "Lord" (*dominus*) as reproachful and insulting. When the words "O just and gracious Lord!" were uttered in a comedy at which he was a spectator and all the people sprang to their feet and applauded as if the words had been directed at him, he at once checked their unseemly flattery by look and gesture, and on the following day sharply reproved them in an edict. After that he would not allow himself to be called "Sire" even by his children or his grandchildren either in jest or earnest, and he forbade them to use such flattering terms even among themselves. He did not if he could help it leave or enter any city or town except in the evening or at night, to avoid disturbing anyone by the obligations of ceremony. In his consulship he commonly went through the streets on foot, and when he was not consul, generally in a closed litter. His morning receptions were open to all, including even commoners, and he met the requests of those who approached him with great affability, jocosely reproving one man because he presented a petition to him with as

---

Suetonius, *Life of Augustus* 53; 55; 79. Based on the translation by J. C. Rolfe, Loeb Classical Library (Cambridge, Mass.: Harvard University Press, 1920).

much hesitation "as he would a penny to an elephant." On the day of a meeting of the Senate he always greeted the members in the House and in their seats, calling each man by name without a prompter; and when he left the House, he used to take leave of them in the same manner, while they remained seated. He exchanged social calls with many, and did not cease to attend all their anniversaries, until he was well on in years and was once inconvenienced by the crowd on the day of a betrothal. When Gallus Cerrinius, a senator with whom he was not at all intimate, had suddenly become blind and had therefore resolved to end his life by starvation, Augustus called on him and by his consoling words induced him to live. . . .

He did not even dread the lampoons against him which were scattered in the Senate house, but took great pains to refute them; and without trying to discover the authors, he merely proposed that thereafter anyone who published pamphlets or slanderous verses under a false name should be investigated. . . .

He was unusually handsome and exceedingly graceful at all periods of his life, though he cared nothing for personal adornment. He was so far from being particular about the dressing of his hair, that he would have several barbers working in a hurry at the same time, and as for his beard he now had it clipped and now shaved, while at the very same time he would either be reading or writing something. His expression, whether in conversation or when he was silent, was so calm and mild, that one of the leading Gauls admitted to his countrymen that it had softened his heart, and kept him from carrying out his design of pushing the emperor over a cliff, when he had been allowed to approach him under the pretense of a conference, as he was crossing the Alps. Augustus had clear, bright eyes, in which he liked to have it thought that there was a kind of divine power, and it greatly pleased him, whenever he looked keenly at anyone, if he let his face fall as if before the radiance of the sun; but in his old age he could not see very well with his left eye. His teeth were wide apart, small, and ill-kept; his hair was slightly curly and inclining to golden; his eyebrows met. His ears were of moderate size, and his nose projected a little at the top and then bent slightly inward. His complexion was between dark and fair. He was short of stature (although Julius Marathus, his freedman and keeper of his records, says that he was five feet and seven inches in height), but this was concealed by the fine proportion and symmetry of his figure, and was noticeable only by comparison with some taller person standing beside him.

15

MACROBIUS

On Augustus' Sense of Humor

Fifth Century CE

Ancient scholars liked to collect anecdotes, quotations, and even jokes about famous men and women. Here the late Roman writer Macrobius brings together from various sources a number of jokes of Augustus— some are really quite funny. He seems to have been able to take a joke on himself.

When Augustus learned that among the children under two years old whom Herod, king of the Jews, had ordered to be executed, the king's own son had died, he said, "I'd rather be Herod's pig than his son."[1] . . .

When Augustus complained that the Tyrian cloth he had bought was too dark, the shopkeeper said, "Hold it higher and look at it from underneath." His answer was witty: "What? Do I have to walk on a balcony to show the Roman people that I am well-dressed?" . . .

A man from the provinces made a bitter joke. He so resembled Caesar that when he came to Rome, everyone stared at him. Augustus ordered the fellow be brought to him and, after looking him over, asked, "Tell me, young man, was your mother ever in Rome?" "No," the man said, but he gleefully added, "but my father often was." . . .

Octavian returned in glory from the victory at Actium. Among the crowd of well-wishers one fellow carried a raven, which he had taught to say "Hail, Caesar, victor, commander!" Caesar was amazed by this loyal bird, and bought it for 20,000 sesterces. A partner of this con man who had received no part of the gift told Caesar that the man had a second raven and asked that he be made to produce it. The bird was brought and spoke the words it had learned: "Hail, victor, commander, Antony!" Caesar was not angry, but he only ordered the man to divide the gift with his partner.

[1]This is an allusion to Jewish kosher practice; if Herod did not eat pork, his pigs were safe.

Macrobius, *Saturnalia* 2, 4, 11; 14; 20; 29–31. Translated by Ronald Mellor, 2004.

Augustus was greeted in a similar way by a parrot and ordered its purchase; he bought a magpie as well. This example persuaded a poor shoemaker to train a raven to say the same greeting. When the bird refused to reply, the impoverished man would say, "I've wasted my money and my work." But when the bird began to give the greeting, Augustus, passing by, heard it and said, "I already have enough flatterers at home." The raven's memory was good enough to add the words it used to hear from its master: "I've wasted my money and my work." At this Caesar roared with laughter and ordered the bird to be purchased at a higher price than any other.

When Caesar used to come down from the Palatine, a Greek would offer an epigram in his honor. He often did this but without success. Augustus saw that he was going to do it again, and he himself hastily scratched a Greek epigram in his own hand on a piece of paper and gave it to the man as they met. The Greek read it, approved it, and showed his approval in his looks and words. When he came to the throne, he plunged his hand into a worn purse and produced a few pennies which he gave to the Emperor and said in Greek, "By your Fortune, Augustus, if I had more I'd have given you more." With everyone laughing, Caesar called his steward and ordered him to pay the poor Greek 100,000 sesterces.

3

The New Constitution

16

CASSIUS DIO

How Agrippa and Maecenas Gave Political Advice to Augustus

Third Century CE

Cassius Dio, writing under the openly tyrannical Severan regime, under-stood that Augustus had created a monarchical government long before the word "king" could be publicly spoken at Rome. He assumed that Augustus must have received guidance from his chief advisors, Agrippa and Maecenas, and constructed a hypothetical debate between them. This sort of imaginary "debate" formed an important element in Greek and Roman rhetorical education. Although the speeches are fictional, the arguments contain many issues that might have been discussed in 28 BCE.

The anachronisms in the two speeches are understandable. For Cassius Dio, who was born during the reign of Marcus Aurelius (161–180 CE), the Empire had brought peace and prosperity. In his own day, it was threatened by German invaders from the north and by Persians to the east. He saw no real alternative to an empire controlled by a strong central government. Although he projected his own concerns two cen-turies into the past, he provided insight into how the ancients might have weighed alternative political structures.

In the first speech, Agrippa makes conventional arguments in support

Cassius Dio, *Roman History* 52, 1–2; 6; 13; 15; 17; 19; 24–25; 27; 40–41. Based on the translation of Earnest Cary, Loeb Classical Library (Cambridge, Mass.: Harvard University Press, 1917).

of the old republican system of government. He uses Greece as an exemplar of democracy. His strongest argument — in retrospect, because Dio had seen it happen — is that conspirators and flatterers will surround the monarch. However, there are thoughtful elements here as well — the fact that people will contribute more in taxes if they have more control. (This realization led to the Magna Carta *in England in 1215.)*

Such were the achievements of the Romans and such their suffering under the kingship, under the Republic, and under the dominion of a few, during a period of seven hundred and twenty-five years. After this they reverted to what was, strictly speaking, a monarchy, although Caesar Augustus planned to lay down his arms and to entrust the management of the state to the Senate and the people. He made his decision, however, in consultation with Agrippa and Maecenas, with whom he used to share all his secret plans; and Agrippa, taking the lead, spoke as follows:

"Be not surprised, Caesar, if I shall try to turn your thoughts away from monarchy, even though I would gain many advantages from it, if it was you who held the position. For if it were to be beneficial to you as well, I should advocate it most earnestly. But the privileges of a monarchy are by no means the same for the rulers as for their friends. On the contrary, jealousies and dangers fall to the lot of the rulers while their friends reap, without incurring either jealousies or dangers, all the benefits they can wish for. So I thought that, in this issue as in all others, I should not be concerned with my own benefit, but for yours and the state's.

"Let us consider, now, at our leisure all the characteristics of this system of government and then shape our course in whichever direction our reason may lead us. For surely no one will assert that we are obliged to choose monarchy in any and all circumstances, even if it be not profitable. If we choose it, people will think that we have fallen victims to our own good fortune and have lost our judgment because of our success, or else that we have been aiming at sovereignty all along. They will think that our appeals to Julius Caesar and our devotion to his memory were mere pretexts and that we used the people and the Senate as a cloak, not intending to free them from those who plotted against them, but of making them slaves to ourselves. And either explanation involves censure for us. For who could help being indignant when he finds that we have said one thing and then discovers that we have meant another? Would he not hate us much more now than if we had at the outset laid bare our desires and set out directly for the monarchy? . . .

"To begin first with the least important consideration, it will be necessary that you procure a large supply of money from all sides; for it is impossible that our present revenues should suffice for the support of the troops, not to speak of the other expenses. Now this need of funds, to be sure, exists in democracies also, since it is not possible for any government to continue without expense. But in democracies many citizens make large contributions, preferably of their own free will, in addition to what is required of them, making it a matter of patriotic emulation and securing appropriate honors in return for their generosity; or, if taxes are also levied on the whole body of citizens, they submit to it both because it is done with their own consent and because the contributions they make are in their own interests. In monarchical governments, on the other hand, the citizens all think that the ruling power alone, to which they credit boundless wealth, should bear the expense; for they are very ready to search out the ruler's sources of income, but not reckon his expenses so carefully; and so they make no contributions from their private means gladly or of their own free will, nor are the public levies they make voted of their own free choice. . . .

"Reflecting upon these considerations and the others which I mentioned a little while ago, be prudent while you may and duly place in the hands of the people the army, the provinces, the offices, and the public funds. If you do it at once and voluntarily, you will be the most famous of men and the most secure; but if you wait for some compulsion to be brought to bear upon you, you will very likely suffer some disaster and gain infamy besides. . . . For it is a difficult matter to induce this city, which has enjoyed a democratic government for so many years and holds empire over so many people, to consent to become a slave to any one. You have heard how the people banished Camillus just because he used white horses for his triumph; you have heard how they deposed Scipio from power, first condemning him for some act of arrogance; and you remember how they proceeded against your father Julius Caesar just because they conceived a suspicion that he desired to be sole ruler. Yet there have never been any better men than these. . . ."

[The long speech of Maecenas, less than a third of which follows, contains elements of a political pamphlet from the third century BCE writ-

ten under the shadow of the tyrannical Caracalla (211–217 CE) and the
insane Elagabalus (218–222 CE). Here, through the imagined speech of
Maecenas, Cassius Dio argues for the ideal kingship long promoted by
ancient philosophers. The emperor, he advises, must respect the senators
and govern humanely. When Cassius Dio warns against "atheists," he
anachronistically may be projecting his concern about Christianity on to
Romans who lived a quarter century before the birth of Jesus.

The speech also includes many anachronisms concerning the reign of
Augustus. Maecenas advises Augustus to create two praetorian prefects,
which was not done until 2 BCE. Many other proposals he makes mirror
Augustus' later policies on taxes and budget, the use of equestrians as a
salaried civil service, and the deployment of the legions. Thus this docu-
ment gives us an excellent picture of what later Romans saw as the
greatest achievements of the first emperor.]

"For I would not have you think that I am advising you to enslave the
people and Senate and then set up a tyranny. I should never dare suggest this to you nor would you ever do it yourself. The other course,
however, would be honorable and expedient both for you and for the
city—that you should yourself, in consultation with the best men,
enact all the appropriate laws, without the possibility of any opposition
to these laws on the part of anyone from the masses; that you and
your counselors should conduct wars according to your own wishes,
that all other citizens should instantly obey your commands; that the
selection of officials should rest with you and your advisers; and that
you and they should also determine the honors and the punishments.
The advantage of all this would be that whatever pleased you in consultation with your peers would immediately become law; that our
wars against our enemies would be waged with secrecy and at the
opportune time; that those to whom any task was entrusted would be
appointed because of their merit and not as the result of ambition for
office; that the good would be honored without arousing jealousy and
the bad punished without causing rebellion. Thus whatever business
was done would be most likely to be managed in the right way, instead
of being referred to the popular assembly, or deliberated upon openly,
or entrusted to partisan delegates, or exposed to the danger of ambitious rivalry. We should be happy in the enjoyment of the blessings given to us, instead of being embroiled in hazardous wars abroad
or in terrible civil strife. For these are the evils found in every democracy—that the powerful try to get supreme power and they hire others—but they have been most frequent in our country, and there is

no other way to put a stop to them than the way I propose. And the evidence is, that we have now for a long time been engaged in wars and civil strife. . . .

"Now I think you have long since been convinced that I am right in urging you to give the people a monarchical government. If this is the case, accept the leadership over them readily and with enthusiasm— or rather do not throw it away. For the question we are deliberating upon is not whether we shall take something, but whether we shall decide not to lose it and by so doing incur danger into the bargain. Who, indeed, will spare you if you thrust the control of the state into the hands of the people, or even if you entrust it to some other man, seeing that there are great numbers whom you have injured, and that practically all these will lay claim to the sovereignty, and yet no one of them will wish either that you should go unpunished for what you have done or that you should be allowed to survive as his rival? . . .

"I maintain, therefore, that you ought first and foremost to choose and select with discrimination the entire senatorial body, inasmuch as some who have not been fit have, on account of our dissensions, become senators. Such of them as possess any excellence you ought to retain, but the rest you should erase from the roll. Do not, however, get rid of any good man because of his poverty, but even give him the money he requires. In the place of those who have been dropped introduce the noblest, the best, and the richest men obtainable, selecting them not only from Italy but also from the allies and the subject nations. In this way you will have many assistants for yourself and will have in safekeeping the leading men from all the provinces; thus the provinces, having no leaders of established repute, will not begin rebellions, and their prominent men will regard you with affection because they have been made sharers in your empire. . . .

"Of the *equites* the two best should command the praetorian body-guard which protects you, for it is hazardous to entrust it to one man, and sure to lead to confusion to entrust it to more than two. Therefore there should be two such commanders, called prefects, in order that, if one of them feels indisposed, you may still not lack a person to guard you. And men should be appointed to this office who have served in many military campaigns and have, besides, held many administrative positions. . . .

"The management of the public funds—I mean both those of the people and those of the empire, not only in Rome but also in the rest of Italy and outside Italy—should be entirely in the hands of the *equites,* and they, as well as all the other members of the equestrian order who are charged with an administrative position, should be on salary, greater or less in proportion to the dignity and importance of their duties. The reason for the second part of this suggestion is that it is not possible for the *equites,* since they are poorer than the senators, to meet their expenditures out of their own means, even when their duties keep them in Rome. . . .

". . . If any of the *equites,* after passing through many branches of the service, distinguishes himself enough to become a senator, his age ought not to hinder him at all from being enrolled in the Senate. Indeed, some *equites* should be received into the Senate, even if they have seen service only as company commanders in the citizen legions, except such as have served in the rank and file. . . .

"A standing army also should be supported, drawn from the citizens, the subject nations, and the allies, its size in the several provinces being greater or less as necessity demands; and these troops ought always to be under arms and to engage in the practice of warfare continually. They should have winter-quarters constructed for them at the most advantageous points, and should serve for a stated period, so that a portion of life may still be left for them between their retirement from service and old age. . . .

"Think upon these things and upon all that I have told you, and be persuaded of me, and let not this fortune slip which has chosen you from all mankind and has set you up as their ruler. For, if you prefer the monarchy in fact but fear the title of 'king' as being accursed, you have but to decline this title and still be sole ruler under the appellation of 'Caesar.' And if you require still other epithets, your people will give you that of 'imperator' as they gave it to your father; and they will pay reverence to your august position by still another term of address, so that you will enjoy fully the reality of the kingship without the odium which attaches to the name of 'king.' "

Maecenas thus brought his speech to an end. And Caesar heartily commended both him and Agrippa for the wealth of their ideas and of their arguments and also for their frankness in expressing them; but he preferred to adopt the advice of Maecenas. He did not, however, immediately put into effect all his suggestions, fearing to meet with failure at some point if he purposed to change the ways of all mankind at a stroke; but he introduced some reforms at the moment and some at a later time, leaving still others for those to effect who should subsequently hold the principate, in the belief that as time passed a better opportunity would be found to put these last into operation. And Agrippa, also, although he had advised against these policies, cooperated with Caesar most zealously in respect to all of them, just as if he had himself proposed them.

17

The Law Bestowing Power on the Emperor
January 70 CE

This extraordinary inscription records the bestowal of imperial power on the emperor Vespasian at the beginning of 70 CE. Although this "law" passed the assembly, it contains the language of a senatorial decree passed a few weeks earlier. It attributes similar powers to earlier emperors, harking back to the time of Augustus, even though no such explicit law would have been passed at that time. This is an indication that the powers of the emperors became more explicit over time.

The bronze tablet on which the inscription is written was found in Rome around 1347 by the revolutionary leader Cola di Rienzi, who set it up for public display. Rienzi used it as propaganda against the popes who then ruled Rome, on the grounds that all power derives from the people. It is still on display in the Capitoline Museum in Rome.

I   ... that it shall be lawful to make a treaty with whomever he wishes, just as it was lawful for the deified Augustus, Tiberius Caesar, and Claudius Caesar.

II   ... And it shall be lawful for him to hold a meeting of the Senate, to make a motion or to refer a matter to it, and to propose decrees of the Senate by a motion and through a vote, as it was lawful for the deified Augustus, Tiberius Caesar, and Claudius Caesar.

III   ... And that when a meeting of the Senate is held in accordance with his wish, or authority, or order, or instruction, or in his presence, the validity of all the actions shall be the same as if the Senate meeting had been convoked and held in accordance with a law.

IV   ... And when he commends to the Senate and people those who are seeking a magistracy, power, *imperium,* or responsibility over anything, and he promises or gives his support to candidates, they will be given extraordinary consideration at the elections.

Inscriptiones Latinae Selectae 244. Edited by H. Dessau, translated by Ronald Mellor, 2004.

V   ... And that it shall be lawful for him to move and extend the boundaries of the *pomerium* [city boundaries] whenever he thinks that it is in the public interest, as it was lawful for Claudius Caesar.

VI   ... And that he will have the right and power to do whatever he thinks is in the public interest, for the majesty of divine and human, public or private affairs, just as the deified Augustus, Tiberius Caesar, and Claudius Caesar had the right.

VII   ... And that, by whatever laws and plebiscites it was written that deified Augustus, Tiberius Caesar, and Claudius Caesar were not bound, the imperator Caesar Vespasian shall be free from those laws and plebiscites, and whatever the deified Augustus, Tiberius Caesar, and Claudius Caesar could do in accordance with a law or proposal, it shall be lawful for the imperator Caesar Vespasian Augustus to do those things.

VIII   ... And whatever, before the passage of this law, has been done, carried out, decreed or ordered by the imperator Caesar Vespasian by his order or instruction, those things in the future will be legal and binding, just as if they had been enacted by a law or plebiscite.

Oath

If anyone due to this law has or shall have acted contrary to laws, proposals, plebiscites, or decrees of the Senate, or if he does not do in consequence of this law anything he must in accordance with a law, proposal, plebiscite, or decree of the Senate, he shall not be punished nor shall he have to pay any penalty to the people, nor shall anyone have the right to bring lawsuit or charges concerning such matter, nor shall any official allow charges before him on this matter.

4

Creating a New Elite:
Senators and Equestrians

18

SUETONIUS

How Augustus Revised the Membership of the Senate

Second Century CE

Suetonius records that Augustus pruned the roll of the Senate in 28 and 18 BCE, purging some of the thugs who had become members during the civil wars. It is clear from the security precautions that he feared violence from those being expelled. Augustus himself says that he revised the senatorial rolls three times (Res Gestae 8) with the third revision in 11 BCE.

Since the number of the senators was swelled by a low-born and ill-assorted rabble—in fact, the Senate numbered more than a thousand, some of whom, called by the vulgar *Orcivi,* were slaves set free by their master's will. They were admitted to the Senate by Marc Antony under pretense that they had been named in the papers left by Caesar, but they were wholly unworthy, and were admitted after Caesar's death through favor or bribery. Augustus restored it to its former limits and distinction by two enrolments, one according to the choice of the members themselves, each man naming one other, and a second made by Agrippa and himself. On the latter occasion it is thought that

---

Suetonius, *Life of Augustus* 35. Based on the translation by J. C. Rolfe, Loeb Classical Library (Cambridge, Mass.: Harvard University Press, 1920).

he wore a coat of mail under his tunic as he presided and a sword by his side, while ten of the most robust of his friends among the senators stood by his chair. Cremutius Cordus writes that even then the senators were not allowed to approach except one by one, and after the folds of their robes had been carefully searched. Some he shamed into resigning, but he allowed even these to retain their distinctive dress, as well as the privilege of viewing the games from the orchestra and taking part in the public banquets of the order. Furthermore, that those who were chosen and approved might perform their duties more conscientiously, and also with less inconvenience, he provided that before taking his seat each member should offer incense and wine at the altar of the god in whose temple the meeting was held; that regular meetings of the Senate should be held not oftener than twice a month, on the Kalends and the Ides; and that in the months of September and October only those should be obliged to attend who were drawn by lot, to a number sufficient for the passing of decrees. He also adopted the plan of privy councils chosen by lot for terms of six months, with which to discuss in advance matters which were to come before the entire body. On questions of special importance he called upon the senators to give their opinions, not according to the order established by precedent, but just as he fancied, to induce each man to keep his mind on the alert, as if he were to initiate action rather than give assent to others.

19

The Town of Superaequum Honors a Local Man Who Became a Senator

Early First Century CE

Throughout Italy many members of locally important families reached the Senate under Augustus. The proud citizens of Superaequum in central Italy honored one of those, Geminus, who was the first senator from their region. Geminus held many of the highest offices, both as praetor at Rome and as proconsul in the provinces.

Inscriptiones Latinae Selectae 932. Edited by H. Dessau, translated by Ronald Mellor, 2004.

To Quintus Varius Geminus, son of Quintus, twice legate of the deified Augustus, proconsul, praetor, tribune of the plebs, quaestor, judicial investigator, prefect for the distribution of grain, member of the commission of ten for deciding disputes, administrator for the maintenance of sacred buildings and public monuments.[1] He was the first of all the Paelignians to be made a senator and to hold these positions. The citizens of Superaequum set this up to their patron from public funds.

[1]Geminus held most of the highest offices in the state. Proconsuls and praetors served as governors in the provinces, while the legate of Augustus commanded a legion. Among the lesser offices, the prefect of the grain supply was especially important because incompetence could result in food shortages and riots.

20

A Town in Asia Honors a Roman Administrator

6 CE

This dedication to Fabricius Tuscus by the city councilors of what was then Alexandria Troas in Asia (built on the supposed site of ancient Troy) demonstrates the extraordinary utility of a skilled equestrian to the emperor. Tuscus was a military tribune—an officer between the senatorial commander and the centurions—and later commanded a unit of auxiliary cavalry. His work in charge of building at Troas must have endeared him to the local citizens. Their inscription dutifully records a series of minor administrative, military, and even religious offices that Tuscus held.

To Gaius Fabricius Tuscus, son of Gaius, of the tribe Aniensis, duumvir[2] augur, prefect of the Apulan cohort and prefect of the building projects carried out in the colony by order of Augustus, military tribune of legion 3 Cyrenaica for eight years, tribune of the conscrip-

[2]A duumvir is one of two chief magistrates in a Roman town.

P. A. Brunt, *Zeitschrift für Papyrologie und Epigraphik* 13 (1974): 161–85. Translated by Ronald Mellor, 2004.

tion of the free-born which Augustus and Tiberius held at Rome, prefect of the engineers for four years, prefect of the cavalry of the praetorian squadron for four years, awarded the honors of the "spear without a point" and the gold crown by Germanicus Caesar, imperator, in the German war. By decree of the city council.

5

Social and Religious Reform

21

SUETONIUS

On How Augustus Must Be Worshipped with the Goddess Roma

Second Century CE

Cities and provinces throughout the Empire included the goddess Roma in their worship of Augustus, but the emperor cautiously avoided such divine honors at Rome.

Although well aware that it was usual to vote temples even to proconsuls, [Augustus] would not accept one even in a province except jointly in his own name and that of Roma. In the city of Rome itself he refused this honor most emphatically, even melting down the silver statues which had been set up in his honor in former times and with the money coined from them dedicating golden tripods to Apollo of the Palatine. When the people did their best to force the dictatorship upon him, he knelt down, threw off his toga from his shoulders and with bare breast begged them not to insist.

Suetonius, *Life of Augustus* 52. Based on the translation by J. C. Rolfe, Loeb Classical Library (Cambridge, Mass.: Harvard University Press, 1920).

22

JOSEPHUS

On King Herod's Construction of a Temple to Roma and Augustus

Late First Century CE

Although Josephus had been the commander of a Jewish army against the Romans during the Great Revolt, he surrendered and went to Rome, where he tried to explain Jewish history and traditions in his book Jewish Antiquities, *written in Greek for an international readership. In it he tells how, between 22 and 10 BCE, King Herod built a lavish Greek-style city on the coast of Judaea, calling it Caesarea after the emperor. It contained, among other elements (a theater, a gymnasium), a temple of Roma and Augustus that must have infuriated observant Jews. The city later became the Roman capital of the province with its military garrison. It remained loyal to Rome during the Jewish revolt in 66 CE. The remains of Caesarea are located just north of Tel Aviv. Its Roman theater is still used for opera performances.*

Now when he saw a place near the sea, which was appropriate for a city, and was previously called Strato's Tower, King Herod set about planning a magnificent city there, and energetically erected everywhere many buildings of white stone. He also adorned it with most sumptuous palaces and large structures for containing the people. And what was the greatest and most laborious work of all, he adorned it with a harbor, that was always free from the waves of the sea. . . .

Now there were buildings all along the circular harbor, made of polished stone, and a certain hill, on which he erected a temple, that was seen a great way off by those that were sailing for that harbor. It had in it two statues, the one of Roma, the other of Caesar. The city, called

Josephus, *Jewish Antiquities* 15, 331–41. Based on the translation by William Whiston (London, 1737).

Caesarea, was also built of fine materials, and had a fine structure. In fact even the subterranean vaults and cellars had no less of architecture bestowed on them than had the buildings above ground. . . .

Herod also built there a theater of stone; and on the south quarter, behind the port, an amphitheater also, capable of holding a vast number of men, and conveniently situated for a view to the sea. So this city was finished in twelve years; during which time the king did not fail to complete with the work, and to pay the charges that were necessary.

23

SUETONIUS

On Augustus' Restoration of Temples and Revival of Religious Rituals

Second Century CE

Suetonius here recounts a number of activities through which Augustus restored neglected rites and religious buildings. Augustus also honored great Romans of the past by placing their statues in the new Forum of Augustus.

After he finally had assumed the office of *pontifex maximus* on the death of Lepidus (for he could not make up his mind to deprive him of the honor while he lived), he collected whatever prophetic writings of Greek or Latin origin were in circulation anonymously or under the names of authors of little repute, and burned more than two thousand of them, retaining only the Sibylline books and making a choice even among those. He deposited these books in two gilded cases under the pedestal of the Palatine Apollo. Inasmuch as the calendar, which had been set in order by the deified Julius, had later been confused and

Suetonius, *Life of Augustus* 31. Based on the translation by J. C. Rolfe, Loeb Classical Library (Cambridge, Mass.: Harvard University Press, 1920).

disordered through negligence, he restored it to its former system; and in making this arrangement he called the month Sextilis by his own surname Augustus, rather than his birth month September, because in the former he had won his first consulship and his most brilliant victories. He increased the number and importance of the priests, and also their allowances and privileges, in particular those of the Vestal virgins. Moreover, when there was occasion to choose another Vestal in place of one who had died, and many used all their influence to avoid submitting their daughters to the hazard of the lot, he solemnly swore that if anyone of his granddaughters were of eligible age, he would have proposed her name. He also revived some of the ancient rites which had gradually fallen into disuse, such as the augury of the goddess Salus [Safety], the priesthood of Jupiter, the ceremonies of the *Lupercalia,* the Secular Games, and the festival of the *Compitalia.*[1] At the *Lupercalia* he forbade beardless youths to join in the running, and at the Secular Games he would not allow young people of either sex to attend any entertainment by night except in company with some adult relative. He provided that the Lares of the Crossroads should be crowned twice a year, with spring and summer flowers.

Next to the immortal Gods he honored the memory of the leaders who had raised the Roman people from obscurity to greatness. Accordingly he restored the works of such men with their original inscriptions, and in the two colonnades of his forum dedicated statues of all of them in triumphal garb, declaring besides in a proclamation: "I have contrived this to lead the citizens to require me, while I live, and the rulers of later times as well, to attain the standard set by those worthies of old." He also moved the statue of Pompey from the hall in which Julius Caesar had been killed and placed it on a marble arch opposite the grand entrance of Pompey's theater.

---

[1]At the *Lupercalia* on February 15, sacrifices and races commemorated the cave where the she-wolf raised Romulus. Augustus held the Secular Games in 17 BCE to commemorate the end of Rome's seventh century, while he revived the *Compitalia* to honor the gods of the crossroads.

24

The City of Narbo Celebrates
the Emperor's Birthday

11 CE

This inscription on an altar erected in honor of Augustus at Narbo (modern Narbonne), in southern Gaul, records the annual celebrations on the emperor's birthday (September 23) and other anniversaries. Similar celebrations were held throughout the Empire.

In the consulship of Titus Statilius Taurus and Lucius Cassius Longinus, on September 22nd, the people of Narbo undertake in perpetuity this vow to the divinity of Augustus:

May it be good, fortunate, and happy for Imperator Caesar Augustus, son of the deified Julius, father of his country, high priest (*pontifex maximus*), in the 34th year of his tribunician power, and for his wife, children, and family, and for the Senate and Roman people, and for the colonists and other inhabitants of Colonia Julia Paterna of Narbo Martius, who have promised to worship his divinity forever. The people of Narbo erected an altar in the forum at Narbo, where each year on September 23rd, on which day the good fortune of our times brought Augustus forth to lead the world, three Roman equestrians, chosen from the people, and three freedmen should each sacrifice a victim and should give to the colonists and other inhabitants on that day, at their own expense, incense and wine for prayers to his divinity; and on September 24th they should likewise give incense and wine to the colonists and inhabitants; on 1st January they should also give incense and wine to the colonists and other inhabitants; also on 7th January, on which day Augustus first took over world power, they should offer a prayer with incense and wine and each sacrifice a victim and on that day give to the colonists and other inhabitants incense and wine; and on 31st May, because on that day, in the consulship of Titus Statilius Taurus and Marius Aemilius Lepidus, he joined the courts of the plebs to the city councilors, they should each sacrifice a victim and give to the colonists and inhabitants incense and wine for prayers to his divinity. . . .

Inscriptiones Latinae Selectae 112. Edited by H. Dessau, translated by Ronald Mellor, 2004.

25

CASSIUS DIO

On Augustus' Speech in Favor of Marriage
Third Century CE

In his Roman History, *Cassius Dio records that Augustus delivered two speeches in the Forum in 11 CE, one to married equestrians and a second, excerpted here, to those who were unmarried. The emperor was distressed that the latter group was larger than the former. Although these speeches are the historian's invention, the arguments in the speeches are plausible. In the second speech, the emperor makes bachelorhood into a moral failing, and urges the* equites *to marry and produce children for the sake of Rome.*

The emperor also proposed legislation to reward those with children. Ironically, the law bore the name of two consuls who were both unmarried.

"Yet, if one were to name the worst crimes, the others are slight in comparison with this one you are now committing, whether you consider them individually or even set all of them together over against this single crime of yours. For you are committing murder in not creating in the first place those who ought to be your descendants; you are committing sacrilege in putting an end to the names and honors of your ancestors; and you are guilty of impiety in that you are abolishing your families, which were instituted by the gods, and destroying the greatest of offerings to them—human life—thus overthrowing their rites and their temples. Moreover, you are destroying the State by disobeying its laws, and you are betraying your country by rendering her barren and childless; in fact, you are destroying Rome by making it empty of future inhabitants. For it is human beings that constitute a city, we are told, not houses or porticos or marketplaces empty of men.

"Consider, therefore, how angry great Romulus, the founder of our people, would be if he could think about his own birth and then upon

Cassius Dio, *Roman History* 56, 5; 7; 9–10. Based on the translation by Earnest Cary, Loeb Classical Library (Cambridge, Mass.: Harvard University Press, 1924).

your conduct in refusing to beget children even by lawful marriages! How angry would his followers be if they knew that, after they themselves had even seized foreign girls, you are not satisfied even with those of your own race, and after they had got children even by enemy wives, you will not beget them even of women who are citizens! . . .

"For surely it is not your delight in solitude that leads you to live without wives, nor is there any one of you who either eats alone or sleeps alone; no, what you want is freedom to be dissolute and lustful. Yet I allowed you to pay your court to girls still of tender years and not yet ripe for marriage, in order that, classed as prospective bridegrooms, you might live as family men should; and I permitted those not in the senatorial order to wed freedwomen, so that, if anyone through love or intimacy should be disposed to such a course, he might go about it lawfully. And I did not limit you rigidly even to this, but at first gave you three whole years in which to make your preparations, and later two. Yet not even so, by threatening, or urging, or postponing, or entreating, have I accomplished anything? For you see for yourselves how much more numerous you are than the married men, when you ought by this time to have provided us with as many children besides, or rather with several times your number. How otherwise can families continue? How can the State be preserved, if we neither marry nor have children? For surely you are not expecting men to spring up from the ground, as happens in mythology, to inherit your property and your public duties. And yet it is neither right nor creditable that our race should cease, and the name of Romans be blotted out with us, and the city be given over to foreigners—Greeks or even barbarians. Do we not free our slaves chiefly for the express purpose of making out of them as many citizens as possible? And do we not give our allies a share in the government in order that our numbers may increase? And do you, then, who are Romans from the beginning and claim as your ancestors the famous Marcii, the Fabii, the Quintii, the Valerii, and the Julii, do you desire that your families and names alike shall perish with you? . . .

"Therefore, fellow-citizens—for I believe that I have now persuaded you both to hold fast to the name of citizens and to secure the title of men and fathers as well—I have administered this rebuke to you not for my own pleasure but from necessity, and not as your enemy nor as one who hates you but rather loving you and wishing to obtain many others like you, in order that we may have lawful homes to dwell in and houses full of descendants, so that we may approach the gods together with our wives and our children, and in partnership with one another may risk our all in equal measure and reap in like degree the hopes we cherish in them. How, indeed, could I be a good ruler over you, if I could endure to see you growing constantly fewer in number? How could I any longer be rightfully called father by you, if you rear no children? Therefore, if you really hold me in affection, and particularly if you have given me this title not out of flattery but as an honor, be eager now to become both men and fathers, in order that you may not only share this title yourselves but may also justify it as applied to me."

Such were his words to the two groups at that time. Afterwards he increased the rewards to those who had children and in the case of the others made a distinction between the married men and the unmarried by imposing different penalties; furthermore, he granted a year's time to those who were remiss in either respect, in which to obey him and thus escape the penalties. . . .

26

ROMAN LAW CODES

Details of Augustan Legislation on Adultery and Marriage

Sixth Century CE

Roman law codes and legal scholarship provide a more precise account of Augustus' legislation to promote marriage and discourage adultery. His goal was to encourage greater fertility among the upper classes. The laws, called "Julian Laws" after Augustus' family name, intruded for the first time into what had been regarded as "private" matters, which had traditionally been resolved by family councils. No penalty was imposed for a Roman man who had sexual relations with a slave, only for a Roman man who had sexual relations with a respectable Roman man or woman. It is uncertain which provisions belong to the original law of 18 BCE and which to the revision of 9 CE.

Justinian, *Institutes* 4, 18, 2–3; Justinian, *Digest* 4, 4, 37; Ulpian, *Epitome* 13–14. Translated by C. H. Monro (Cambridge: Cambridge University Press, 1904).

A. Public prosecutions are as follows . . . the "Julian Law for the suppression of adultery" punishes with death not only those who dishonor the marriage bed of another but also those who indulge in unspeakable lust with males. The same Julian Law also punishes the offence of seduction, when a person, without the use of force, corrupts a virgin or seduces a respectable widow. The penalty imposed by the statute on such offenders is the confiscation of half their estate if they are of respectable standing, corporal punishment and banishment in the case of people of the lower orders.

B. But as regards the provisions of the Julian Law . . . a man who confesses that he has committed the adultery has no right to ask for a remission of the penalty on the ground that he was under age; nor, as I have said, will any remission be allowed if he commits any of those offences which the statute punishes in the same way as adultery; as, for example, if he marries a woman who is detected in adultery and he declines to divorce her, or where he makes a profit from her adultery, or accepts a bribe to conceal illicit intercourse which he detects, or lends his house for the commission of adultery or illicit intercourse within it; youth, as I said, is no excuse in the face of clear enactments, when a man who, though he appeals to the law, himself transgresses it.

C. By the terms of the "Julian Law on marriage," senators and their descendants are forbidden to marry freedwomen, or women who have themselves followed the profession of the stage, or whose father or mother has done so; other freeborn persons are forbidden to marry a common prostitute, or a procuress, or a woman manumitted by a procurer or procuress, or a woman caught in adultery, or one condemned in a public lawsuit, or one who has followed the profession of the stage. . . .

27

Funeral Oration for an Exceptional Wife
Late First Century BCE

This inscription, usually called the "Laudatio Turiae," is the longest private Latin inscription that has survived. In it a bereaved husband extols his late wife for her traditional virtues of loyalty and chastity. He also praises her extraordinarily brave actions during the civil wars and proscriptions of the 40s BCE. After he was condemned, she managed to hide and protect him until Octavian issued a pardon and even personally confronted the triumvir Lepidus. When the couple could not have children, the wife encouraged him to divorce her for a wife who could provide children. The husband says he angrily refused.

The woman and her husband are unknown; those details may have been in the lost section of the text. The text is in the form of a funeral oration. The text provides a rare insight into an amazing personal relationship that comes alive after two thousand years.

The day before our wedding you were suddenly left an orphan when both your parents were murdered. Although I had gone to Macedonia and your sister's husband, Gaius Cluvius, had gone to the province of Africa in 49 BCE, the murder of your parents did not remain unavenged. You carried out this act of piety with such great diligence—asking questions, making inquiries, demanding punishment that if we had been there, we could not have done better. You and that very pious woman, your sister, share the credit for success. . . .

Rare indeed are marriages of such long duration, which are ended by death, not divorce. We had the good fortune to spend forty-one years together with no unhappiness. I wish that our long marriage had come finally to an end by my death, since it would have been more just for me, who was older, to yield to fate.

Why should I mention your personal virtues—your modesty, obedience, affability, and good nature, your tireless attention to woolworking, your performance of religious duties without superstitious

Translated by Jo-Ann Shelton, *As the Romans Did,* 2nd ed. (Oxford: Oxford University Press), No. 330, pp. 292–94.

fear, your artless elegance and simplicity of dress? Why speak about your affection toward your relatives, your sense of duty toward your family (for you cared for my mother as well as you cared for your parents)? Why recall the countless other virtues which you have in common with all Roman matrons worthy of that name? The virtues I claim for you are your own special virtues; few people have possessed similar ones or been known to possess them. The history of the human race tells us how rare they are.

When my political enemies were hunting me down, you aided my escape by selling your jewelry; you gave me all the gold and pearls which you were wearing and added a small income from household funds. We deceived the guards of my enemies, and you made my time in hiding an "enriching" experience. . . .

Why should I now disclose memories locked deep in my heart, memories of secret and concealed plans? Yes, memories—how I was warned by swift messages to avoid present and imminent dangers and was therefore saved by your quick thinking; how you did not permit me to be swept away by my foolhardy boldness; how, by calm consideration, you arranged a safe place of refuge for me and enlisted as allies in your plans to save me, your sister and her husband, Gaius Cluvius, even though the plans were dangerous to all of you. If I tried to touch on all your actions on my behalf, I could go on forever. For us let it suffice to say that you hid me safely.

Yet the most bitter experience of my life came later. . . . I was granted a pardon by Augustus, but his colleague Lepidus opposed the pardon. When you threw yourself on the ground at his feet, not only did he not raise you up, but in fact he grabbed you and dragged you along as if you were a slave. You were covered with bruises, but with unflinching determination you reminded him of Augustus Caesar's edict of pardon. . . . Although you suffered insults and cruel injuries, you revealed them publicly in order to expose him as the author of my calamities. . . .

When the world was finally at peace again and order had been restored in the government, we enjoyed quiet and happy days. We longed for children, but spiteful fate begrudged them. If Fortune had allowed herself to care for us in this matter as she does others, we two would have enjoyed complete happiness. But advancing old age put an end to our hopes for children. . . . You were depressed about your infertility and grieved because I was without children. . . . You spoke of divorce and offered to give up your household to another woman, to a fertile woman. You said that you yourself would arrange for me a new wife, one worthy of our well-known love, and you assured me that you would treat the children of my new marriage as if they were your own. You would not demand the return of your inheritance; it would remain, if I wished, in my control. You would not detach or isolate yourself from me; you would simply carry out henceforth the duties and responsibilities of my sister or my mother-in-law.

I must confess that I was so angered by your suggestion that I lost my mind. I was so horrified that I could scarcely regain control of myself. How could you talk of a dissolution of our marriage before it was demanded by fate! How could you even conceive in your mind of any reason why you should, while still alive, cease to be my wife, you who remained very faithfully with me when I was in exile, indeed almost in exile from life! How could the desire or need for having children be so great that I would break faith with you! . . .

I wish that our old age had allowed our marriage to last until I, who was the elder, had passed away; it would have been fairer for you to arrange a funeral for me. . . . But by fate's decree, you finished the race of life before I did, and you left me all alone, without children, grieving and longing for you. . . . But inspired by your example I will stand up to cruel fortune, which has not stolen everything from me since it allows the memory of you to grow brighter and stronger through praise. . . .

I conclude my oration with this: you have deserved all, and I can never repay you completely. I have always considered your wishes my commands. I will continue to do for you whatever I still can.

May the Spirits of the Dead grant to you and protect your eternal peace, I pray.

28

DIONYSIUS OF HALICARNASSUS

On How the Emancipation of Roman Slaves Corrupts the Citizen Body

8 BCE

The Greek orator and historian Dionysius came to Rome in 30 BCE. His Roman Antiquities is a long history of Rome from its foundations down to 264 BCE, but he also included comments on Rome of his own day. Because Greeks regarded freed slaves as foreigners rather than citizens, Dionysius is shocked that the Romans allow all freed slaves to immediately become Roman citizens and he graphically describes the many abuses that resulted from this practice.

Things have come to such a state of confusion and the noble traditions of the Roman commonwealth have become so debased and sullied, that some who have made a fortune by robbery, housebreaking, prostitution and every other base means, purchase their freedom with the money so acquired, and immediately become Roman citizens. Others, who have been confidants and accomplices of their masters in poisonings, murders and in crimes against the gods or the state, receive from them this favor as their reward. Some are freed in order that, when they have received the monthly grain allowance given by the public, or some other hand-outs distributed by the politicians to the poor citizens, they may bring it to those who granted them their freedom. And others owe their freedom to the flippancy of their masters and to their eagerness for popularity. I, at any rate, know of some who have allowed all their slaves to be freed after their death, in order that they might be called good men when they were dead and that many people might walk in their funeral processions wearing their liberty-caps;[2] indeed, some of those taking part in these processions, as one

---

[2]Former slaves wore a conical hat, called a liberty cap, to show their status.

Dionysius, *Roman Antiquities* 1, 24, 4–6. Based on the translation of Earnest Cary, Loeb Classical Library (Cambridge, Mass.: Harvard University Press, 1937).

might have heard from those who knew, have been criminals just out of jail, who had committed crimes deserving a thousand deaths. Most people, nevertheless, as they look upon these stains that can scarce be washed away from the city, are grieved and condemn the custom, looking upon it as tasteless that a dominant city which aspired to rule the world should make such men citizens.

29

GAIUS

On Augustan Laws Restricting the Freeing of Slaves

Second Century CE

Augustus passed a series of laws to restrict manumission—the freeing of slaves—to control the abuses mentioned by Dionysius. The Roman jurist Gaius, in his textbook of Roman law called The Institutes, *describes the key elements of these laws. The* lex Aelia Sentia *of 4 CE does not prohibit the manumission of misbehaving slaves, but it also does not allow them to become Roman citizens. The law also prohibits the freeing of slaves under the age of thirty in a will, and it does not allow owners under the age of twenty to free slaves at all.*

In the lex Fufia Caninia *of 2 BCE, Augustus fixed precise limits on manumission in a will—never more than one hundred slaves. Private property was important to the Romans and they were suspicious of state interference, so owners could in fact free all their slaves during their lifetimes. However, the emperor was attempting to control emotional deathbed decisions to liberate hundreds—perhaps even thousands—of slaves who would all receive Roman citizenship.*

I   The *lex Aelia Sentia* enacts that slaves who have been punished by their proprietors with chains or have been branded, or have been

Gaius, *The Institutes* 1, 13; 18; 40; 42–45. Adapted from the translation by E. Poste (Oxford: Clarendon Press, 1904).

examined under torture on a criminal charge, and have been convicted, or have been condemned to fight with men or beasts, or have been committed to gladiatorial school or a public prison, if subsequently manumitted by the same or by another proprietor, shall acquire by manumission the status of surrendered enemies. . . .

II   The requirement of an age of the slave was introduced by the *lex Aelia Sentia,* by the terms of which law, unless he is thirty years old, a slave cannot on manumission become a citizen of Rome, unless the form of manumission is by *vindicta,*[3] preceded by proof of adequate motive before the council. . . .

III   Since the *lex Aelia Sentia* imposes a certain restriction on manumission for owners under the age of twenty, it follows that, though a person who has completed his fourteenth year is competent to make a will, and therein to name an heir and make bequests; yet, if he has not attained the age of twenty, he cannot therein free a slave. . . .

IV   By the *lex Fufia Caninia,* a certain limit is fixed to the number of slaves who can receive manumission in a will. An owner who has more than two slaves and not more than ten is allowed to free as many as half that number; he who has more than ten and not more than thirty is allowed to free a third of that number; he who has more than thirty and not more than a hundred is allowed to free a quarter; lastly, he who has more than a hundred and not more than five hundred is allowed to free a fifth; and, however many a man possesses, he is never allowed to manumit more than this number, for the law prescribes that no one shall free more than a hundred. On the other hand, if a man has only one or two, the law is not applicable, and the owner has unrestricted power of manumission.

Nor does the statute apply to any but testamentary manumission, so that by the form of *vindicta* or inscription on the censor's register, or by attestation of friends, a proprietor of slaves may free his whole household, provided that there is no other let or hindrance to prevent their manumission.

---

[3]Manumission by *vindicta* referred to the staff with which the owner touched each slave before the magistrate in the act of liberation. During a census, conducted each five years, the owner could also declare slaves free.

6

The Army in War and Peace

30

VELLEIUS PATERCULUS

On the Annihilation of Rome's German Legions
First Century CE

Quinctilius Varus, who became governor of Germany, owed his promotion to two fortunate marriages—one to a daughter of Agrippa and another to a great-niece of Augustus. He was, together with Tiberius, consul for 13 BCE. He served as governor in Africa and in Syria before being sent to Germany in 9 CE, where he lost three legions in the ambush in the Teutoburg Forest.

Although some scholars believe that Varus was made a scapegoat for a failure of imperial policy, we see in this excerpt of Velleius Paterculus the official position on the disaster: blame Varus! Velleius had served under Tiberius and his history shows him to be intensely loyal to the regime. If, as Velleius suggests, Varus was a corrupt governor of Syria, why did Augustus send him to the dangerous province of Germany? Whether the defeat was a failure of Varus' judgment or of imperial policy, it determined that the Rhine would remain the boundary of the Empire for centuries.

Quinctilius Varus was born of a noble rather than an illustrious family. He was of a mild disposition, of sedate manners, and since he was rather lazy as well, in body as in mind, he was more accustomed to

Velleius Paterculus, *Compendium of Roman History* II, 117–19. Adapted from the translation by John S. Watson (London: G. Bell and Sons, 1881).

ease in a camp than to action in the field. How far he was from despising money, Syria, of which he had been governor, afforded proof; for, going a poor man into that rich province, he became a rich man, and left it a poor province. Being appointed commander of the army in Germany, he imagined that the inhabitants had nothing human but the voice and limbs, and that men who could not be tamed by the sword, might be civilized by law. With this notion, having marched into the heart of Germany, as if among people who enjoyed the pleasure of peace, he spent the summer deciding controversies, and judging the cases brought to court.

But those people, though a person unacquainted with them would hardly believe it, are, while extremely savage, exquisitely artful, a race, indeed, formed by nature for deceit. Accordingly, by introducing fictitious disputes one after another, by sometimes prosecuting each other for pretended injuries, and then returning thanks for the decision of these suits by Roman equity, for the civilization of their barbarous state by this new system, and for the determination by law of disputes which used to be determined by arms, they at length lulled Quinctilius into such a perfect feeling of security, that he fancied himself a city magistrate giving justice in the forum, instead of the commander of an army in the middle of Germany.

It was at this time that a youth of illustrious birth, the son of Segimer, prince of that nation, named Arminius, brave in action, intelligent, and of mental activity much above the state of barbarism, showing in his eyes and face the passion of his feelings. This youth had constantly accompanied our army in the previous war, and had obtained Roman citizenship, and the rank of an equestrian. He took advantage of the general's laziness to perpetrate an act of atrocity, shrewdly judging that no man is more easily cut off than he who feels no fear, and that false security often leads to disaster. At first he shared his thoughts with a few, and afterward to more, stating to them, and assuring them, that the Romans might be cut off by surprise. He then proceeded to add action to resolution, and fixed a time for carrying a plot into action. Notice of this intention was given to Varus by Segestes, a man of that nation, worthy of credit, and of high rank; but the warnings did not change destiny which had already darkened the mental vision of the Roman general. . . . Varus refused to believe the information, asserting that he felt a trust in the good will of the people, proportioned to his kindness toward them. However, after this first premonition, there was no time left for a second.

The circumstances of this dreadful calamity—the worst to befall the Romans in a foreign country, since the destruction of Crassus in

Parthia, I will tell in my larger history. At present we can only lament the whole. An army unrivaled in bravery, the flower of the Roman troops in discipline, vigor, and experience in war, was brought, through the spinelessness of its leader, the treachery of the enemy, and the cruelty of Fortune, into a desperate situation. The men could not even fight their way out, as they wished, some being even severely punished by the general, for using Roman arms with Roman spirit. So they were hemmed in by woods, lakes, and the enemy in ambush, and were entirely cut off by those enemies whom they had before slaughtered like cattle, and of whose life and death had been subject to the mercy or severity of the Romans.

The leader showed some spirit in dying, though none in fighting; for, imitating the example of his father and grandfather, he ran himself through with his sword. . . . The savage enemy mangled the half-burned body of Varus; his head was cut off, and brought to the chieftain Marobodus, and being sent by him to Caesar, was at length honored with burial in the sepulcher of his family.

31

SUETONIUS

On Augustus' Reaction to News of the Disaster in Germany
Second Century CE

This is a dramatic account of the emperor's response to the disaster in Germany. Regardless of whether all the details are true, the defeat cast a shadow over the last years of Augustus' reign.

He suffered only two shameful defeats, those of Lollius and Varus, both of which were in Germany. Of these the former was more humiliating than serious, but the latter was almost fatal, since three legions were cut to pieces with their general, his lieutenants, and all the auxiliaries.

Suetonius, *Life of Augustus* 23. Based on the translation by J. C. Rolfe, Loeb Classical Library (Cambridge, Mass.: Harvard University Press, 1920).

When the news of this came, he ordered that watch be kept by night throughout the city, to prevent any outbreak, and he prolonged the terms of the governors of the provinces, that the allies might be held to their allegiance by experienced men with whom they were acquainted. He also vowed great games to Jupiter Optimus Maximus, in case the condition of the commonwealth should improve, a thing which had been done in the Cimbric and Marsic wars. In fact, they say that he was so greatly affected that for several months in succession he cut neither his beard nor his hair, and sometimes he would dash his head against a door, crying: "Quinctilius Varus, give me back my legions!" And he observed the day of the disaster each year as one of sorrow and mourning.

7
Italy and the Provinces

32

TACITUS

On the Administration of the Empire
Second Century CE

In his summary of the administration of the Empire in his Annals, *Tacitus gives an overly favorable account of the state of the provinces. It is impossible, for example, to believe that corporal punishment was unknown only five years before the crucifixion of Jesus. Rather, Tacitus is painting a particularly rosy picture for rhetorical purposes, because he wishes to emphasize the effect of the accession of the cruel praetorian prefect Sejanus, who became in 24 CE the emperor Tiberius' chief advisor. For Tacitus, the administration of the provinces had obviously improved under Augustus and Tiberius, and the new government diminished the greed and violence of Roman administration under the Republic.*

I think this is a convenient opportunity for me to review the earlier prevailing methods of administration in the other departments of the State, inasmuch as that year [24 CE] brought with it the beginning of a change for the worse in Tiberius's policy. In the first place, public business and the most important private matters were managed by the Senate: the leading men were allowed freedom of discussion, and when they stooped to flattery, the emperor himself checked them. He bestowed honors with regard to noble ancestry, military renown, or

---

Tacitus, *The Annals* 4, 6. Adapted from the translation by A. J. Church and W. J. Brodribb (London: Macmillan, 1886).

brilliant accomplishments as a civilian, letting it be clearly seen that there were no better men to choose. The consul and the praetor retained their prestige; inferior magistrates exercised their authority; the laws too, with the single exception of cases of treason, were properly enforced.

As to the taxes on grain, the indirect taxes and other branches of the public revenue, they were in the hands of companies of Roman *equites.* The emperor entrusted his own property to men of the most obvious integrity or to persons known only by their general reputation, and once appointed they were retained without any limitation, so that most of them grew old in the same employment. The city populace indeed suffered much from high prices, but this was no fault of the emperor, who actually endeavored to counteract barren soil and stormy seas with every resource of wealth and foresight. And he was also careful not to distress the provinces by new burdens, and to see that in bearing the old they were safe from any rapacity or oppression on the part of governors. Corporal punishments and confiscations of property were unknown.

33

SUETONIUS

On How Augustus Showed Great Respect for Greek Culture

Second Century CE

This anecdote presents Augustus, just before his death, showing respect for the culture of his provincial subjects. While wealthy Romans did not wear Greek clothing in Rome, they enjoyed "playing the Greek"—as they called it—when relaxing at their villas on the Bay of Naples.

Then after skirting the coast of Campania and the neighboring islands, he spent four more days at his villa in Capri, where he gave himself up

---

Suetonius, *Life of Augustus* 98. Based on the translation by J. C. Rolfe, Loeb Classical Library (Cambridge, Mass.: Harvard University Press, 1920).

wholly to rest and social diversions. As he sailed by the gulf of Puteoli it happened that from an Alexandrian ship which had just arrived there, the passengers and crew, clad in white, crowned with garlands, and burning incense, lavished upon him good wishes and the highest praise, saying that it was through him that they lived, through him that they sailed the seas, and through him that they enjoyed their liberty and their fortunes. Exceedingly pleased at this, he gave forty gold pieces to each of his companions, exacting from every one of them a pledge under oath not to spend the sum that had been given them in any other way than in buying wares from Alexandria. More than that, for the several remaining days of his stay, among little presents of various kinds, he distributed togas and cloaks as well, stipulating that the Romans should use the Greek dress and language and the Greeks the Roman.

34

CASSIUS DIO

On How Augustus "Shared"
Provincial Government with the Senate

Third Century CE

In this document, Dio reports Augustus' willingness to keep control of certain provinces—namely, the ones with a substantial military presence—after the Senate refused his offer in 27 BCE to resign all his powers. The senatorial provinces were governed by proconsuls; the imperial provinces by the emperor's deputies called "legates of Caesar." Dio makes it clear that he regarded this distinction as a sham.

In this way he had his supremacy ratified by the Senate and by the people as well. But since he still wished to be thought to be democratic, while he accepted all the oversight of the public business, on the ground that it required some attention on his part, yet he declared

---

Cassius Dio, *Roman History* 53, 12–13; 15. Based on the translation by Earnest Cary, Loeb Classical Library (Cambridge, Mass.: Harvard University Press, 1924).

he would not personally govern all the provinces, and that in the case of such provinces as he should govern he would not do so indefinitely. He did, in fact, restore to the Senate the weaker provinces, on the ground that they were free from war, while he retained the more powerful, alleging that they were insecure and precarious and either had enemies on their borders or were able on their own account to begin a serious revolt. His professed motive in this was that the Senate might fearlessly enjoy the finest portion of the Empire, while he himself had the hardships and the dangers; but his real purpose was that by this arrangement the senators will be unarmed and unprepared for battle, while he alone had arms and maintained soldiers. Africa, Numidia, Asia, Greece with Epirus, the Dalmatian and Macedonian districts, Crete and the Cyrenaic portion of Libya, Bithynia with Pontus which adjoined it, Sardinia and Baetica were held to belong to the people and the Senate; while to Caesar belonged the remainder of Spain—that is, the district of Tarraco and Lusitania—and all the Gauls—that is, Gallia Narbonensis, Gallia Lugdunensis, Aquitania, and Belgica, both the natives themselves and the aliens among them. For those Celts, whom we call Germans, had occupied all the Belgic territory along the Rhine and caused it to be called Germany, the upper portion extending to the sources of that river, and the lower portion reaching to the British Ocean. These provinces, then, together with Syria, Phoenicia, Cilicia, Cyprus and Egypt, fell at that time to Caesar's share; for afterwards he gave Cyprus and Gallia Narbonensis back to the people, and for himself took Dalmatia instead. . . .

Such, then, was the apportionment of the provinces. And wishing, even then, to lead the Romans a long way from the idea that he was at all monarchical in his purposes, Caesar undertook for only ten years the government of the provinces assigned him; for he promised to reduce them to order within this period, and boastfully added that, if they should be pacified sooner, he would the sooner restore them, to the Senate. Thereupon he first appointed the senators themselves to govern both classes of provinces, except Egypt. This province alone he assigned to an equestrian, the one we have already named, for the reasons mentioned there. . . .

This is the system followed in the case of the provinces of the people. To the others, which are called the imperial provinces and have more than one citizen-legion, are sent officials who are to govern them as legates appointed by the emperor himself, generally from those who had already served as praetors in Rome. . . .

35

Imperial Edicts for the Government of Cyrene
7 BCE

Augustus issued a series of edicts concerning the province of Cyrene (modern Libya), which was nominally under the rule of a senatorial proconsul. These edicts demonstrate the emperor's resolve to remedy problems in remote provinces, even those he claimed he had "returned to the Senate."

Several edicts concerned jury service and citizenship. There had obviously been a conflict between the native Greeks and Roman citizens living there, with Romans bringing charges against the Greeks. In the first edict, the emperor shows his concern with the judicial process regarding capital crimes, because a very small number of Roman citizens formed the jury pool and innocent Greeks had been convicted and executed. The emperor proposes that a Greek defendant in a capital case could choose to have a half-Greek jury. In the fourth edict, the emperor specifies that in noncapital cases, the jury could be fully Greek.

These six Cyrene edicts survive on an inscription found in 1926.

I   Emperor Caesar Augustus, *pontifex maximus,* holding the tribunician power for the seventeenth time, saluted imperator for the fourteenth time, proclaims:

Since I find that in the province of Cyrene there are altogether 215 Roman citizens of every age whose census rating is 2,500 denarii or more, and that the jurors are drawn from this number in which several cliques are known to exist, and since the delegations coming from the cities of the province have complained that these cliques are unfair to Greeks in capital crimes, when the same people act as prosecutors and as witnesses for each other in turn, and since I myself have learned that some innocent persons have been overwhelmed in this way and have suffered the death penalty, until the Senate decides on

From *Ancient Roman Statutes: A Translation, with Introduction, Commentary, Glossary, and Index,* translated by A. C. Johnson, P. R. Coleman-Norton, and F. C. Bourne (Austin: University of Texas Press, 1961).

this point or I myself find some better remedy, it appears to me that the governors of Crete and Cyrene will do wisely and fittingly, if they appoint in the province of Cyrene an equal number of jurors from both Greeks and Romans of greatest wealth and not less than twenty-five years of age, having a census rating and property of not less than 7,500 denarii, if a sufficient number of such men can be found, or, if the number of jurors to be placed on the public list cannot be provided in this way, they shall post as jurors citizens who have half of this amount of wealth and not less than half to sit on capital cases involving Greeks.

If a Greek is brought to trial, he shall have the right, on the day before his accuser speaks, to determine whether he wishes his jury to be all Roman or half Greek. If he chooses the latter, then an equal number of balls shall be assigned to each Greek and Roman and their names shall be written on them. The names of the Romans shall be drawn by lot from one urn, and those of the Greeks from the other, until a panel of twenty-five is drawn from each group. The prosecutor, if he wishes, may reject one from each group; the defendant may reject three in all, provided that he does not reject all Roman or all Greek. Then the remainder shall be set aside for jury duty. They shall be separated for voting and shall cast their votes separately, the Romans in one urn, the Greeks in another. Then, when the votes are counted separately, whatever the majority declare the governor publicly shall pronounce as the verdict. Since for the most part relatives of the deceased do not suffer an unjust death to remain unavenged and since it is unlikely that Greek accusers for relatives or fellow citizens who have been slain will be lacking in exacting punishment from the accused, it appears to me that the governors of Crete and Cyrene will do rightly and properly, if they do not permit in the province of Cyrene a Roman to accuse a Greek for the murder of a Greek man or woman, unless some Greek who has been granted Roman citizenship brings an action for the death of some kinsman or fellow citizen. . . .

IV   Emperor Caesar Augustus, *pontifex maximus,* holding the tribunician power for the seventeenth time, proclaims:

Except for suits involving the death penalty, which the governor himself shall conduct and upon which he shall pronounce judgment, or for which he shall appoint a panel of jurors, in suits which arise between Greeks in the province of Cyrene for all other matters, it is my pleasure that Greeks shall be appointed as jurors, unless the accused or the defendant wishes to have Roman citizens as jurors, but for those to whom Greeks are given by this my decree it is my pleasure that no juror shall be appointed from that city to which the plaintiff or the defendant also belongs. . . .

36

JOSEPHUS

On Augustus' Confirmation
of the Rights of Jewish Communities
Late First Century CE

Several sources indicate that Jewish communities in the East complained to Rome when Greek cities interfered with their privileges—especially the right to send a temple tax to Jerusalem. Augustus confirmed this right for Jewish cities in Asia in 2 CE—when Censorinus was governor of that province.

This text was among a number of documents concerning Jewish privileges that the pro-Roman Jewish historian Josephus has collected. Jews and Greeks were among the most literate of the peoples conquered by Rome, so we find in their writings reactions to their treatment by Augustus.

Now the cities of Asia ill-treated the Jews, and also those who lived in Libya, which joins to Cyrene, where the former kings had given them equal privileges with the other citizens. But the Greeks outraged them at this time, took away their religious contributions, and did harm to them. When the Jews were thus harmed, and found no end of their barbarous treatment they suffered from the Greeks, they sent ambassadors to Caesar to complain, and he granted them the same privileges as they had before, and sent letters to the same purpose to the governors of the provinces, copies of which I attach here, as evidence of the former favorable attitude the Roman emperors had towards us.

"Caesar Augustus, high priest and tribune of the people, ordains thus: Since the nation of the Jews has been grateful to the Roman

Josephus, *Jewish Antiquities* 16, 6, 1–2. Translated by William Whitson (London, 1737).

people, not only now, but in the past as well, and especially Hyrcanus
the high priest, under my father Julius Caesar, it seemed good to me
and my advisors, according to the sentence and oath of the people of
Rome, that the Jews have liberty to live by their own customs, according to the law of their forefathers, as they did under Hyrcanus the
high priest of the Almighty God. Their religious contributions be not
touched, but be sent to Jerusalem, and that it be committed to the
care of the treasurers at Jerusalem. Jews should not be obliged to go
before any judge on the Sabbath day, nor on the day of the preparation
to it, after the ninth hour. But if any one be caught stealing their holy
books, or their religious contributions, whether it be out of the syna-
gogue or public school, he shall be deemed a sacrilegious person, and
his goods shall be brought into the public treasury of the Romans.
And I order that the evidence which they have given me, on account
of my regard to that piety which I exercise toward all mankind, and
out of regard to Caius Marcus Censorinus, together with the present
decree, be proposed in that most eminent place which has been consecrated to me by the community of Asia at Ancyra. And if any one
transgress any part of what is above decreed, he shall be severely punished." This was inscribed upon a pillar in the temple of Caesar.

37

PHILO OF ALEXANDRIA

On Augustus' Benevolence toward Rome's Jews
39 CE

*In his speech to the emperor Caligula (37–41 CE), the Jewish philoso-
pher Philo harkened back to Augustus' concern for the Jews of Rome who
lived across the Tiber in what is today called Trastevere. Philo, who lived
his first thirty-eight years in the reign of Augustus, confirmed Josephus'
texts, which reflected an imperial policy sympathetic to Jewish concerns.
The Jews of Rome continued to live in Trastevere until the Middle Ages,
when the popes moved them into the Ghetto.*

Philo, *Legation to Gaius* 155–58. Based on the translation by Charles Yonge (London:
G. Bell and Sons, 1854).

How then did Augustus look upon the large area of Rome across the river Tiber, which he was well aware was occupied and inhabited by the Jews? And they were mostly Roman citizens, having been emancipated; for, having been brought as captives into Italy, they were freed by those who had bought them for slaves, without ever having been compelled to alter any of their hereditary or national observances.

Therefore, he knew that they had synagogues, and that they were in the habit of visiting them, and most especially on the sacred Sabbath days, when they publicly cultivate their own religion. He knew also that they were in the habit of making religious contributions of money and sending them to Jerusalem by the hands of those who were to conduct the sacrifices.

But he never removed them from Rome, nor did he ever deprive them of their rights as Roman citizens, because he had a regard for Judaea. Nor did he ever meditate any changes with respect to their synagogues, nor did he forbid their assembling for the interpretation of the law, nor did he make any opposition to their offerings of first fruits. But he behaved with such piety toward our countrymen, and with respect to all our customs, that he, I may almost say, with all his family, adorned our temple with many costly and magnificent offerings, commanding that continued sacrifices of burnt offerings should be offered up for ever and ever every day from his own revenues, as a dedication of his own to the most high God. These sacrifices are performed to this very day, and will be performed for ever, as a proof of a truly imperial attitude.

Moreover, in the monthly distributions, when the whole people receives money or grain in turn, he never allowed the Jews to be deprived of their share of this favor. Even if it happened that this distribution fell on the day of their sacred Sabbath, on which day it is not lawful for them to receive anything, or to give anything, or in short to perform any of the ordinary duties of life, he gave special instructions to make the distribution to the Jews on the day following, that they might not lose the effects of his general generosity.

38

THE GOSPEL ACCORDING TO LUKE

On the Birth of Jesus of Nazareth
About 80 CE

In the years after the crucifixion of Jesus of Nazareth, called "The Christ," his disciples wrote accounts of his life called "gospels." The Gospel According to Luke was attributed to a Jewish doctor who wrote it in Greek. There is one point of confusion, as there is no record of a universal census at the time of Jesus' birth in 4 BCE. Most likely it was a census ordered by Quirinius, the governor of Syria, who claimed he was doing it on the authority of the emperor. The local population could hardly distinguish between local orders and commands from Rome; they all came from the provincial governor and all had to be obeyed.

At that time it came to pass that a decree went out from Caesar Augustus, that the whole world should be registered. This was the first census made when Quirinius was governor of Syria. Everyone went to register, each to his own city. Joseph also went up from the city of Nazareth in Galilee, into Judaea, to the city of David, which is called Bethlehem (because he was of the house and family of David), to enroll himself with his wife Mary, who was pregnant with a child. And it came to pass that, while they were there, her time for delivery came due. And she gave birth to her first son; and she wrapped him in swaddling clothes, and laid him in a manger, because there was no room for them in the inn.

Luke, *Gospel According to St. Luke* 2, 1–7.

8

The Imperial Family and Succession

39

SUETONIUS

On the Grandchildren of Augustus

Second Century CE

Throughout history many kings and emperors have found it easier to rule an empire than to control their own families. In the case of Augustus, a combination of bad luck (Gaius' and Lucius' early deaths) and perhaps his own insensitivity in pushing his daughter Julia into political marriages caused him great distress. However, he was remarkably fortunate in having an intelligent, a loyal, and a supportive wife in Livia, whose two sons (Tiberius and Drusus) were both excellent generals in Augustus' service. In his Life of Augustus, Suetonius records the fate of the emperor's five grandchildren.

From Agrippa and Julia, Augustus had three grandsons, Gaius, Lucius, and Agrippa Postumus, and two granddaughters, Julia and Agrippina. He married Julia to Lucius Paulus, the censor's son, and Agrippina to Germanicus, his sister's grandson. Gaius and Lucius he adopted at home, privately transferring them from their father,[1] and initiated them into administrative life when they were still young, sending them to the provinces and the armies as consuls-elect. In bringing up his

---

[1]Roman adoption could be conducted privately or at a public meeting of the assembly.

Suetonius, *Life of Augustus* 64–65. Based on the translation by J. C. Rolfe, Loeb Classical Library (Cambridge, Mass.: Harvard University Press, 1920).

daughter and his granddaughters he even had them taught spinning and weaving, and he forbade them to say or do anything except openly and such as might be recorded in the household diary. He was most strict in keeping them from meeting strangers, once writing to Lucius Vinicius, a young man of good position and character: "You have acted presumptuously in coming to our villa at Baiae to call on my daughter." He taught his grandsons reading, swimming, and the other elements of education, for the most part by himself, taking special pains to train them to imitate his own handwriting; and he never dined in their company unless they sat beside him on the lowest couch, or made a journey unless they preceded his carriage or rode close by it on either side.

But at the height of his happiness and his confidence in his family's development, Fortune proved fickle. He found the two Julias, his daughter and granddaughter, guilty of every form of vice, and banished them. He lost Gaius and Lucius within the span of eighteen months, for the former died in Lycia and the latter at Marseilles. He then publicly adopted his third grandson Agrippa Postumus and at the same time his stepson Tiberius by a bill passed in the assembly; but he soon disowned Agrippa because of his crudity and violent temper, and sent him off to Sorrento. He bore the death of his relatives with far more resignation than their misconduct. For he was not greatly broken by the fate of Gaius and Lucius, but he informed the Senate of his daughter's fall through a letter read in his absence by an official, and for very shame would meet no one for a long time, and even thought of putting her to death. At all events, when one of her confidantes, a freedwoman called Phoebe, hanged herself at about that same time, he said: "I would rather have been Phoebe's father." After Julia was banished, he denied her the use of wine and every form of luxury, and would not allow any man, slave or free, to come near her without his permission, and then not without being informed of his stature, complexion, and even of any marks or scars upon his body. It was not until five years later that he moved her from the island of Pandataria to the mainland and treated her with somewhat less harshness. But he could not by any means be prevailed on to recall her altogether, and when the Roman people several times interceded for her and urgently pressed their suit, he in open assembly called upon the gods to curse them with like daughters and like wives. He would not allow the child born to his granddaughter Julia after her sentence to be recognized or reared. As Agrippa Postumus grew unmanageable, and even became madder from day to day, he transferred him to an island and also set a guard of soldiers over him. He also provided by a decree of the Senate that he should be confined there for all time, and at every mention of him and of the Julias he would sigh deeply and even cry out: "Would that I never had wedded and would I had died without offspring" [*Iliad* III.40]; and he never alluded to them except as his three boils and his three ulcers.

40

TACITUS

On Augustus, Livia, and Their Family
Second Century CE

Tacitus' hostility to Tiberius and his mother Livia is clear in his account of Augustus' family. Here he implies that Livia may have been responsible for the deaths of Gaius and Lucius, as well as for the murder of Agrippa Postumus after the death of Augustus. It seems unlikely that Augustus would have been so naïve as to overlook the deaths of his beloved Gaius and Lucius.

Meanwhile Augustus, as support for his rule, raised to the priesthood and magistracy Claudius Marcellus, his sister's son, while a teenager, and Marcus Agrippa, of humble birth, a good soldier, and one who had shared his victory, to two consecutive consulships. When Marcellus soon afterwards died, the emperor also took Agrippa as his son-in-law. Tiberius Nero and Claudius Drusus, his stepsons, he honored with imperial titles, although his own family was still intact. For he had adopted the children of Agrippa, Gaius and Lucius, into his own family; and before they had yet laid aside the dress of boyhood he had most fervently desired, with an outward show of reluctance, that they should be entitled "princes of the youth," and be consuls-elect. After Agrippa died, and Lucius Caesar as he was on his way to our armies in

Tacitus, *Annals* 1, 3–5. Adapted from the translation by A. J. Church and W. J. Brodribb (London: Macmillan, 1886).

Spain, and Gaius while returning from Armenia, still suffering from a wound, were prematurely cut off by destiny, or by their stepmother Livia's treachery, Drusus too having long been dead, Tiberius remained alone of the stepsons, and on him everything converged. He was adopted as a son, as a colleague in empire and a partner in the tribunitian power, and paraded through all the armies, no longer by his mother's secret intrigues, but at her open suggestion. For she had gained such a hold on the aged Augustus that he drove out as an exile into the island of Planasia, his only grandson, Agrippa Postumus, who, though devoid of worthy qualities, and having only the brute courage of physical strength, had not been convicted of any serious offense. And yet Augustus had appointed Drusus' son Germanicus, to the command of eight legions on the Rhine, and required Tiberius to adopt him, although Tiberius still had a son, now a young man, in his house. Augustus did it that he might have several precautions to rely on. He had no war on his hands at the time except against the Germans, which was rather to wipe out the disgrace of the loss of Quinctilius Varus and his army than out of an ambition to extend the Empire, or for any adequate recompense. At home all was tranquil, and magistrates held the old titles; there was a younger generation, born since the victory of Actium, and even many of the older men had been born during the civil wars. How few were left who had seen the Republic!

Thus the State had been revolutionized, and there was not a vestige left of the old sound morality. Stripped of equality, all looked up to the commands of a sovereign without any anxiety for the present, while Augustus in the vigor of life, could maintain his own position, that of his house, and the general tranquility. When in advanced old age, he was worn out by a weak constitution, and the end was near and new prospects opened, a few spoke in vain of the blessings of freedom, but most people dreaded and some longed for civil war. The popular gossip of the large majority fastened itself variously on their future masters. "Agrippa was savage, and had been enraged by insults, and neither from age nor experience in affairs was he equal to so great a burden. Tiberius was mature, and had succeeded in war, but he had the old inbred arrogance of the Claudian family, and many symptoms of a cruel temper, though they were repressed, now and then broke out. He had also from earliest infancy been reared in an imperial house; consulships and triumphs had been heaped on him in his youth; even in the years which, on the pretext of seclusion he spent in exile at Rhodes, he had had no thoughts but of rage, hypocrisy, and secret lust. There was his mother too with feminine flightiness. The

Roman people must, it seemed, be subject to a female and to two youths besides, who for a while would burden, and some day tear apart the State."

While these and similar topics were discussed, the infirmities of Augustus increased, and some suspected guilt on his wife's part. For a rumor had gone abroad that a few months earlier he had sailed to Planasia on a visit to Agrippa, with the knowledge of some chosen friends, and with one companion, Fabius Maximus. Many tears were shed on both sides, with expressions of affection, and that thus there was a hope of the young man being restored to the home of his grandfather. This, it was said, Maximus had divulged to his wife Marcia, she again to Livia. All was known to Caesar, and when Maximus soon afterwards died, by a death some thought to be self-inflicted, there were heard at his funeral wailings from Marcia, in which she reproached herself for having been the cause of her husband's destruction. Whatever the facts were, when Tiberius was entering Illyria he was summoned home by an urgent letter from his mother, and it is still uncertain whether at the city of Nola he found Augustus still breathing or quite lifeless. For Livia had surrounded the house and its approaches with a strict watch, and favorable bulletins were published from time to time, till, provision having been made for the demands of the crisis, a single report told men that Augustus was dead and that Tiberius was master of the State.

41

AULUS GELLIUS

A Letter from Augustus to His Grandson Gaius
Second Century CE

If Augustus worried about his grandsons being spoiled, he needed to look no further than himself. This letter was written to Gaius, who was about twenty years old, in 1 BCE—three years before his death. The letter was preserved verbatim by the second-century Roman scholar Aulus Gellius

Aulus Gellius, *Noctes Atticae* 15, 7, 3. Translated by Ronald Mellor, 2004.

in his collection of stories called Attic Nights. *Although ancient historians would usually not bother to copy the exact text of a letter, the librarian Suetonius did, as did the linguist Gellius.*

Greetings, my dear Gaius, my delightful little donkey. By Jupiter, I always miss you when you're away from me! But especially on days like today, my eyes need to see my Gaius. Wherever you are today, I hope you are happy and well enough to celebrate my 64th birthday. As you see, I have escaped that 63rd year, a critical point for all old men. And I pray to the gods that, in whatever time is remaining to me, you and I may live in good health with the state flourishing, while you exercise your virtue and succeed to my position.

42

CASSIUS DIO

How Livia Gives Advice to Augustus
Third Century CE

Augustus is believed to have relied heavily on the advice of Livia in matters of state. Although Roman women usually spoke out only within the family circle, some earlier women had also had a significant impact on public events. Nevertheless, there was often suspicion of such behavior. Later sources both record Livia's influence and speculate, at times, about her murderous ambition on behalf of her son Tiberius.

These excerpts are drawn from a lengthy imaginary discussion in 4 BCE between Livia and Augustus on the treatment of conspirators. Livia is portrayed as a prudent counselor, until the ironic turn of the last line, which suggests that she was accused of murdering Augustus.

While he was thus occupied, various men formed plots against him, notably Gnaeus Cornelius, a son of the daughter of Pompey the Great.

Cassius Dio, *Roman History* 55, 14; 16; 21–22. Based on the translation by Earnest Cary, Loeb Classical Library (Cambridge, Mass.: Harvard University Press, 1917).

Augustus was consequently in great perplexity for some time, since he neither wished to put the plotters to death, inasmuch as he saw that no greater safety would accrue to him by their destruction, nor to let them go, for fear this might induce others to conspire against him. While he was in doubt what to do and was finding it impossible either to be free from fear by day or from restlessness by night, Livia one day said to him: "What means this, husband? Why is it that you do not sleep?"

And Augustus answered: "What man, wife, could even for a moment forget his cares, who always has so many enemies and is so constantly the object of plots by one group of men or another? Do you not see how many are attacking both me and our rule? And not even the punishment of those who are brought to justice can stop them, but quite the opposite is true: those who remain are as eager to accomplish their own destruction also as if they were striving for some honorable thing. . . ."

"You are indeed right," answered Livia, "and I have some advice to give you—that is, if you are willing to receive it, and will not criticize me because I, though a woman, dare suggest to you something which no one else, even of your most intimate friends, would venture to suggest—not because they are not aware of it, but because they are not bold enough to speak."

"Speak out," replied Augustus, "whatever it is."

"I will tell you," said Livia, "without hesitation, because I have an equal share in your blessings and your ills, and as long as you are safe I also have my part in reigning, whereas if you come to any harm (which Heaven forbid!), I shall perish with you. . . .

"Let us make the experiment, therefore, beginning with these very men. Perhaps they may not only be reformed themselves, but also make others better; for you see that Cornelius is both of good birth and famous, and we ought, I presume, to take human nature into account in working out such matters. The sword, surely, cannot accomplish everything for you—it would indeed be a great boon if it could bring men to their senses and persuade them or even compel them to love a ruler with genuine affection—but instead, while it will destroy the body of one man, it will alienate the minds of the rest. . . ."

Augustus heeded these suggestions of Livia and released all the accused with some words of admonition; and he even appointed Cornelius consul. As a result of this course he so conciliated both him and the other persons so treated that neither they nor any one of the rest thereafter either actually plotted against him or was suspected of doing so. It was rather Livia herself, who was chiefly responsible for saving the life of Cornelius, who was to be charged with plotting the death of Augustus.

43

SUETONIUS

A Report on Letters
between Augustus and Tiberius
Second Century CE

Because frequent rumors circulated that Augustus did not like Tiberius, Suetonius used his position as imperial archivist to collect passages from the emperor's letters to his stepson. These letters are indeed full of praise, but we must remember how much Augustus needed Tiberius' military skills—especially late in his life—so the flattery may not necessarily be sincere.

I also am aware that some have written that Augustus so openly and unreservedly disapproved of Tiberius' austere manners, that he sometimes broke off his freer and lighter conversation when Tiberius appeared; but that overcome by his wife's entreaties he did not reject his adoption, or perhaps was even led by selfish considerations, that with such a successor he himself might one day be more regretted. But after all I cannot be led to believe that an emperor of the utmost prudence and foresight acted without consideration, especially in a matter of such great importance. It is my opinion that after weighing the faults and merits of Tiberius, he decided that the latter were greater, especially since he took oath before the people that he was adopting Tiberius for the good of the country, and alludes to him in several letters as a most able general and the sole defense of the Roman people. In illustration of both these points, I append a few extracts from these letters:

"Fare thee well, Tiberius, most charming of men, and success go with you, as you war for me and for the Muses. Fare thee well, most charming and valiant of men and most conscientious of generals, or may I never know happiness."

Suetonius, *Life of Tiberius* 21. Based on the translation of J. C. Rolfe, Loeb Classical Library (Cambridge, Mass.: Harvard University Press, 1920).

"I have only praise for the conduct of your summer campaigns, dear Tiberius, and I am sure that no one could have acted with better judgment than you did amid so many difficulties and such apathy of your army. All who were with you agree that the well-known line could be applied to you: 'One man alone by his foresight has saved our dear country from ruin.'"

"If anything comes up that calls for careful thought, or if I am upset at anything, I long mightily, so help me Heaven, for my dear Tiberius, and the lines of Homer come to my mind: 'Let him but follow and we too, though flames round about us be raging, Both may return to our homes, since great are his wisdom and knowledge.'"

"When I hear and read that you are worn out by constant hardships, may the Gods curse me if my own body does not wince in sympathy; and I beg you to spare yourself, that the news of your illness may not kill your mother and me, and endanger the Roman people in the person of their future ruler."

"It matters not whether I am well or not, if you are not well."

"I pray the Gods to preserve you to us and to grant you good health now and forever, if they do not utterly hate the people of Rome."

44

SUETONIUS

Augustus Asks Livia: "What Should We Do about Claudius?"

Second Century CE

These endearing family letters of 12 CE show Augustus struggling with Livia's grandson Claudius, who at this point is twenty-one years old. As a child, Claudius had probably suffered from polio, which left him with a limp, a stutter, and a noticeable twitch. Augustus is torn between his concern for the young man and his fear that he will disgrace his family in public.

Suetonius, *Life of Claudius* 4. Based on the translation by J. C. Rolfe, Loeb Classical Library (Cambridge, Mass.: Harvard University Press, 1920).

Because Claudius was later regarded as feeble-minded and harmless, he survived while his uncle Tiberius murdered other members of the family. He succeeded his nephew Caligula to the throne in 41 CE and ruled well for thirteen years.

Finally, to make it clear what opinions, favorable and otherwise, his great uncle Augustus had of Claudius, I have appended extracts from his own letters: "I have talked with Tiberius, my dear Livia, as you requested, with regard to what is to be done with your grandson Claudius at the games of Mars. Now we are both agreed that we must decide once and for all what plan we are to adopt in his case. For if he be healthy and so to say 'all there,' what reason do have we for doubting that he ought to be promoted through the same positions through which his brother Germanicus has been advanced? But if we realize that he lacks soundness of body and mind, we must not furnish the means of ridiculing both him and us to a public which is accustomed to deride such things. Surely we shall always be in a quandary, if we deliberate about each separate occasion and do not make up our minds in advance whether we think he can hold public office or not. However, as to the matters about which you ask my present advice, I do not object to his having charge of the banquet of the priests at the games of Mars, if he will allow himself to be advised by his relative the son of Silvanus, so as not to do anything to make himself conspicuous or ridiculous. That he should view the games in the circus from the Imperial box does not meet with my approval; for he will be conspicuous if exposed to full view in the front of the auditorium. I am opposed to his going to the celebrations on the Alban Mount, or being in Rome on the days of the Latin festival. For, if he is able to attend his brother on the Mount, why should he not also serve as prefect of the city? You have my views, my dear Livia, namely that I desire that something be decided once and for all about the whole matter, to save us from constantly wavering between hope and fear. Moreover, you may, if you wish, give this part of my letter to his mother, our relative Antonia, to read.

Again in another letter: "I certainly shall invite young Claudius to dinner every day during your absence, to keep him from dining alone with his friends Sulpicius and Athenodorus. I do wish that he would choose more carefully and in a less scatterbrained fashion someone he could imitate in his movements, bearing, and walk. The poor fellow is unlucky; for in important matters, where his mind does not wander, the nobility of his character is apparent enough." Also in a third letter: "Confound me, dear Livia, if I am not surprised that your grandson Claudius could please me with his public speaking. How in the world anyone who is so unclear in his conversation can speak with clearness and propriety when he declaims, is more than I can understand."

9

"City of Marble"—Augustan Culture

45

HORACE

I Came, I Fought, I Ran

23 BCE

When the poet Horace was a student in Athens, he was recruited by Brutus to fight for "freedom" and he formed part of the republican army at Philippi in 42 BCE. In this poem addressed to his friend, Horace says he dropped his shield and fled the battlefield. Did he really? The poem is an imitation of the Greek poet Archilochus, who says he dropped his shield in a battle not far from Philippi 600 years earlier! Because ancient poets often imitated earlier themes, we cannot be certain if Horace's story is history or a poetic conceit.

My friend, who fought with me in extreme danger under our
    general Brutus,
Who restored you to citizenship, your native gods, and the
    Italian sky.
Pompey, my best friend with whom I often whiled away a lazy
    day with wine,
Crowning my glistening hair with Syrian perfumes.

With you I experienced the headlong rout at Philippi, where I
    dropped my shield,

Horace, *Odes* 2, 7. Translated by Ronald Mellor, 2004.

A disgrace! Courage failed, and fierce combatants shamefully bit
    the dust.
I was terrified, but Mercury hid me in a cloud and carried me
    through the enemy,
But the tide of war sucked you back again into the battle.

So give Jove his promised feast, and stretch your tired legs
    under the laurel tree,
And don't leave the cups reserved for you. Fill them with
    numbing Massic wine!
Pour perfume out of vials! Who will weave garlands of parsley or
    myrtle?
Whom will the dice name the master of revels? I will celebrate as
    madly as any Thracian!
It's wonderful to have a wild party when a friend has returned.

46

HORACE

Rejoice: The Egyptian Queen Is Dead
23 BCE

*This poem celebrates the triple triumph of Illyria, Actium, and Egypt,
which Augustus celebrated in 29 BCE. Is even the great poet Horace
guilty of propaganda, or was the Roman elite genuinely relieved at the
end of decades of civil war? The final stanza pays tribute to the queen:
"This was no coward." Her pride and her courage to commit suicide
were both qualities a Roman would genuinely admire.*

Horace, *Odes* 1, 37. Translated by Ronald Mellor, 2004.

Now we must drink, my comrades, and beat the earth with
    dancing;
Now we should decorate the couches of the gods with Salian
    feasts.
Before it would have been a scandal to drink our vintage
    Caecuban wine,
While the mad queen planned to destroy our Capitol and our
    Empire.

With her disgusting gang of perverts, she was so drunk on good
    fortune
That she hoped to take all power.
But when scarcely one ship escaped destruction from the fire,
Caesar turned her mind, soused with Mareotic wine, to terrible
    reality.

His ships pursued as she fled from Italy, as a hawk chases a
    gentle dove,
Or as the swift hunter chases the hare on the snowy fields of
    Thessaly.
He wanted to put that cursed monster in chains, but she wanted
    to die nobly;
She showed no feminine fear of the sword, nor sought to flee
    into hiding.

She dared to look calmly on her ruined palace, and bravely held
    the asps,
To commit a heroic suicide by drawing their black poison into
    her body.
This was no coward! She scorned the notion of being carried—
    no longer a queen—
On enemy ships to adorn another's proud triumph.

HORACE

Augustus Has Brought Peace

13 BCE

Not only did the Golden Age of Latin poetry occur in the reign of Augustus, most of these poets were his friends. Do we read in their praise of the emperor flattery or sincere praise? Although Horace became a friend of Augustus, he turned down a post as his secretary to retain his independence. Here Horace extols the peace that Augustus brought to the Empire, and in the fourth line makes his famous reference to what we call the Age of Augustus: "Caesar, your age."

When I wish to sing of battles and captured cities,
Phoebus Apollo strikes his lyre loudly
And forbids me from going to sea with tiny sails.

Caesar, your age has restored the rich fruit to the fields,
And to Jupiter the standards recaptured from the proud
    Parthians,
And closed the temple of Janus, now free of war. . . .

While Caesar guards our state,
Neither civil war, nor violence, nor that anger
That brings forth swords and besets pitiable towns,
None will drive out our peace.

Horace, *Odes* 4, 15, lines 1–9; 16–20. Translated by Ronald Mellor, 2004.

VIRGIL

A Description of the Battle of Actium
19 BCE

In this passage of Virgil's Aeneid, *the goddess Venus comes to earth with beautiful armor made for her son Aeneas. The shield bears images of the history of Rome and the descendants of Aeneas. In this scene from the shield, Aeneas' heir, Augustus, confronts Antony and Cleopatra at the battle of Actium in 31 BCE. Here Virgil imitates the shield made for Achilles in Homer's* Iliad. *As in Homer, the gods engage in warfare in support of humans.*

Virgil had left instructions that his unfinished epic be burned in the event of his death, but Augustus countermanded his friend's order, preserving for posterity the greatest poem in Latin.

In the middle were the bronze-armored fleets at the battle of Actium. There before your eyes the battle was drawn up with the whole of the headland of Leucas seething and all the waves gleaming in gold. On one side was Augustus Caesar, leading the men of Italy into battle alongside the Senate and the People of Rome, its household gods, and its great gods. High he stood on the poop of his ship while from his radiant forehead there streamed a double flame and his father's star shone above his head. On the other wing, towering above the battle as he led his ships in line ahead, sailed Agrippa with favoring winds and favoring gods, and the beaks of captured vessels flashed from the proud honor on his forehead, the Naval Crown. On the other side, with the wealth of the barbarian world and warriors in all kinds of different armor, came Antony in triumph from the shores of the Red Sea and the peoples of the East. With him sailed Egypt and the power of the East from as far as distant Bactria, and there bringing up the rear was the greatest outrage of all, his Egyptian wife! On they came at speed, all together, and the whole surface of the sea was churned to

Virgil, *Aeneid* 8, 676–708. Adapted from the translation by David West (New York: Penguin Books, 1990).

foam by the pull of their oars and the bow-waves from their triple beaks. They steered for the high sea and you would have thought that the Cycladic Islands had been torn loose again and were floating on the ocean, or that mountains were colliding with mountains, to see men in action on those ships with their massive, turreted sterns, showering blazing torches of tow and flying steel as the fresh blood began to redden the furrows of Neptune's fields. In the middle of all this the queen summoned her warships by rattling her Egyptian drums—she was not yet seeing the two snakes there at her back— while the dog-god Anubis barked and all manner of monstrous gods leveled their weapons at Neptune and Venus and Minerva. There in the eye of battle raged Mars, engraved in iron, the grim Furies swooped from the sky and jubilant Discord strode along in her torn cloak with Bellona at her heels cracking her bloody whip. But high on the headland of Actium, Apollo saw it all and was drawing his bow. In terror at the sight the whole of Egypt and of India, all the Arabians and all the Shebans were turning tail and the queen herself could be seen calling for winds and setting her sails by them.

49

OVID

On Jupiter's Praise of Augustus

8 CE

Ovid ends his great mythological poem, the Metamorphoses, *with a hymn in praise of Augustus. Julius Caesar is already a god, but he is being surpassed by his son Augustus. When Venus expresses her fears for her descendants, Jupiter assures her that Augustus will avenge his father and continue to defeat all his enemies before turning to government. The poet summarizes the battles of Augustus at Mutina, Philippi, and Actium. Despite this praise, the emperor later banned Ovid from Rome for an indiscreet poem (perhaps concerning the emperor's daughter).*

Ovid, *Metamorphoses* 15, 745–55; 794–822. Translated by Brookes More (Boston: Cornhill Publishers, 1922).

Apollo's son came to us from abroad,
but Caesar is a god in his own land.
The first in war and peace, he rose by wars,
which closed in triumphs, and by civic deeds
to glory quickly won, and even more
his offspring's love exalted him as a new,
a heavenly, sign and brightly flaming star.
Of all the achievements of great Julius Caesar
not one is more ennobling to his fame
than being father of his glorious son. . . .

The valiant son will plan revenge on those
who killed his father and will have our aid
in all his battles. The defeated walls
of scarred Mutina, which he will besiege,
shall sue for peace. Pharsalia's plain will dread
his power and Macedonian Philippi
be drenched with blood a second time, the name
of one acclaimed as "Great" shall be subdued
in the Sicilian waves. Then Egypt's queen,
wife of the Roman general, Antony,
shall fall, while vainly trusting in his word,
while vainly threatening that our Capitol
must be submissive to Egypt's power.
Why should I mention all the barbarous lands
and nations east and west by ocean's rim?
Whatever habitable earth contains
shall bow to him, the sea shall serve his will! . . .

With peace established over all the lands,
he then will turn his mind to civil rule
and as a prudent legislator will
enact wise laws. And he will regulate
the manners of his people by his own
example. Looking forward to the days
of future time and of posterity,
he will command the offspring born of his
devoted wife, to assume the imperial name
and the burden of his cares. Nor till his age
shall equal Nestor's years will he ascend
to heavenly dwellings and his kindred stars.

50

VITRUVIUS

On How Augustus Was Patron of the Arts
23 BCE

The architect and engineer Vitruvius forms a bridge between Augustus as patron of literature and Augustus as builder. Here he explicitly thanks Augustus for his patronage, as the emperor's financial support enabled him to write On Architecture — *perhaps the single most influential book on architecture ever written. The architect also recognizes the emperor as perhaps the greatest builder Rome had yet seen.*

While your divine intelligence and will, Imperator Caesar, were engaged in acquiring the right to command the world, and while your fellow citizens, when all their enemies had been laid low by your invincible valor, were glorying in your triumph and victory—while all foreign nations were in subjection awaiting your beck and call, and the Roman people and Senate, released from their alarm, were beginning to be guided by your most noble conceptions and policies, I hardly dared, in view of your serious employments, to publish my writings and long considered ideas on architecture, for fear of subjecting myself to your displeasure by an unseasonable interruption.

But when I saw that you were giving your attention not only to the welfare of society in general and to the establishment of public order, but also to the providing of public buildings intended for utilitarian purposes, so that not only should the State have been enriched with provinces by your means, but that the greatness of its power might likewise be attended with distinguished authority in its public buildings, I thought that I ought to take the first opportunity to lay before you my writings on this theme. . . .

Owing to this favor I need have no fear of want to the end of my life, and being thus laid under obligation I began to write this work for you, because I saw that you have built and are now building extensively, and

---

Vitruvius, *On Architecture* 1, preface 1–3. Translated by Morris Morgan (Cambridge, Mass.: Harvard University Press, 1914).

that in future also you will take care that our public and private buildings shall be worthy to go down to posterity by the side of your other
splendid achievements. I have drawn up definite rules to enable you,
by observing them, to have personal knowledge of the quality both of
existing buildings and of those which are yet to be constructed. For in
the following books I have disclosed all the principles of the art.

51

SUETONIUS

On the Emperor as a Builder
Second Century CE

---

*Augustus not only built temples and public buildings throughout the city,
he also contributed to other urban improvements: building roads, clear-
ing the Tiber, creating a fire brigade, and instituting neighborhood
administrators.*

He built many public works, in particular the following: his forum with
the temple of Mars the Avenger, the temple of Apollo on the Palatine,
and the temple of Jupiter the Thunderer on the Capitol. His reason for
building the forum was the increase in the number of the people and
of cases at law, which seemed to call for a third forum, since two were
no longer adequate. Therefore it was opened to the public with some
haste, before the temple of Mars was finished, and it was provided
that the public prosecutions be held there apart from the rest, as well
as the selection of jurors by lot. He had made a vow to build the
temple of Mars in the war of Philippi, which he undertook to avenge
his father; accordingly he decreed that in it the Senate should consider wars and claims for triumphs, from it those who were on their
way to the provinces with military commands should be escorted, and
to it victors on their return should bear the tokens of their triumphs.

Suetonius, *Life of Augustus* 29–30. Translated by J. C. Rolfe, Loeb Classical Library
(Cambridge, Mass.: Harvard University Press, 1920).

He reared the temple of Apollo in that part of his house on the Palatine for which the soothsayers declared that the god had shown his
desire by striking it with lightning. . . .

He divided the area of the city into regions and wards, arranging
that the former should be under the charge of magistrates selected
each year by lot, and the latter under *magistri* elected by the inhabitants of the respective neighborhoods. To guard against fires he
devised a system of stations of night watchmen, and to control the
floods he widened and cleared out the channel of the Tiber, which had
for some time been filled with rubbish and narrowed by jutting buildings. Further, to make the approach to the city easier from every
direction, he personally undertook to rebuild the Flaminian Road all
the way to Ariminum, and assigned the rest of the highways to others
who had been honored with triumphs, asking them to use their prize-
money in paving them. He restored sacred edifices which had gone to
ruin through lapse of time or had been destroyed by fire, and adorned
both these and the other temples with most lavish gifts, depositing in
the shrine of Jupiter Capitolinus as a single offering sixteen thousand
pounds of gold, besides pearls and other precious stones to the value
of fifty million sesterces.

52

STRABO

A Greek View of Augustan Rome
20 CE

In this excerpt of his Geography, *the Greek geographer Strabo describes
to his Greek readers Augustan Rome as he saw it soon after the
emperor's death. He emphasizes the practical nature of early Romans in
focusing on roads, sewers, and the water supply, then turns to the beautification of Rome under Augustus.*

Strabo, *Geography* 5, 3. Rev. J. Arkenberg. From W. S. Davis, *Readings in Ancient History,* vol. 2 (Boston: Allyn and Bacon, 1912).

The Greek cities are thought to have flourished mainly on account of the felicitous choice made by their founders, in regard to the beauty and strength of their sites, their proximity to some haven, and the fineness of the country. But the Roman prudence was more particularly employed on matters which have received but little attention from the Greeks—such as paving their roads, constructing aqueducts, and sewers. In fact they have paved the roads, cut through hills, and filled up valleys, so that the merchandise may be conveyed by carriage from the ports. The sewers, arched over with hewn stones, are large enough in parts for actual hay wagons to pass through, while so plentiful is the supply of water from the aqueducts, that rivers may be said to flow through the city and the sewers, and almost every house is furnished with water pipes and copious fountains.

We may remark that earlier Romans bestowed little attention upon the beautifying of Rome. But their successors, and especially those of our own day, have at the same time embellished the city with numerous and splendid objects. Pompey, the Deified Caesar, and Augustus, with his children, friends, wife, and sister have surpassed all others in their zeal and munificence in these decorations. The greater number of these may be seen in the Campus Martius which to the beauties of nature adds those of art. The size of the plain is remarkable, allowing chariot races and the equestrian sports without hindrance, and multitudes exercise themselves with ball games, in the circus, and on the wrestling grounds. The structures that surround the campus, the greensward covered with herbage all the year around, the summit of the hills beyond the Tiber, extending from its banks with panoramic effect, present a spectacle which the eye abandons with regret.

Near to this plain is another surrounded with columns, sacred groves, three theaters, an amphitheater, and superb temples, each close to the other, and so splendid that it would seem idle to describe the rest of the city after it. For this cause the Romans esteeming it the most sacred place, have erected funeral monuments there to the illustrious persons of either sex. The most remarkable of these is that called the "Mausoleum" of Augustus which consists of a mound of earth raised upon a high foundation of white marble, situated near the river, and covered on the top with evergreen shrubs. Upon the summit is a bronze statue of Augustus Caesar, and beneath the mound are the funeral urns of himself, his relatives, and his friends. Behind is a large grove containing charming promenades. In the center of the Campus Martius is the spot where the body of Augustus was reduced to ashes. It is surrounded by a double enclosure, one of marble, the other of iron, and planted within with poplars. If you proceed from there to visit the ancient Forum, which is equally filled with basilicas, porticoes, and temples, you will there behold the Capitol, the Palatine, and the noble works that adorn them, and the piazza of Livia, each successive work causing you speedily to forget that which you have seen before. Such then is Rome!

In Rome there is continual need of wood and stone for ceaseless building caused by the frequent falling down of houses, and on account of fires and of remodeling which seem never to cease. Remodeling is a kind of voluntary destruction of houses, each owner knocking down and rebuilding according to his individual taste. For these purposes the numerous quarries, forests, and rivers in the region which convey the materials, offer wonderful facilities.

Augustus Caesar endeavored to avert from the city the dangers alluded to, and instituted a company of freedmen, who should be ready to lend their assistance in the case of conflagration, while as a preventive against falling houses he decreed that all new buildings should not be carried to the same height as formerly, and those erected along the public ways should not exceed seventy feet in height. But these improvements must have ceased except for the facilities afforded to Rome by the quarries, the forests, and the ease of transport.

10

The Death and Legacy of Augustus

53

SUETONIUS

On the Death and Funeral of Augustus

Second Century CE

Suetonius provides a dramatic account of the death and funeral of Augustus.

On the last day of his life he asked every now and then whether there was any disturbance without on his account; then calling for a mirror, he had his hair combed and his falling jaws set straight. After that, calling in his friends and asking whether it seemed to them that he had played the comedy of life fitly, he added the tag: "Since well I've played my part, all clap your hands / And from the stage dismiss me with applause." Then he sent them all off, and while he was asking some newcomers from the city about the daughter of Drusus, who was ill, he suddenly passed away as he was kissing Livia, uttering these last words: "Live mindful of our wedlock, Livia, and farewell," thus blessed with an easy death and such a one as he had always longed for. For almost always on hearing that anyone had died swiftly and painlessly, he prayed that he and his might have a like *euthanasia,* for that was the term he was wont to use. He gave but one single sign of wandering before he breathed his last, calling out in sudden terror that forty young men were carrying him off. And even this was rather

Suetonius, *Life of Augustus* 99–100. Based on the translation of J. C. Rolfe, Loeb Classical Library (Cambridge, Mass.: Harvard University Press, 1920).

a premonition than a delusion, since it was that very number of soldiers of the praetorian guard that carried him forth to lie in state.

He died in the same room as his father Octavius, in the consulship of two Sextuses, Pompeius and Appuleius, on the fourteenth day before the Kalends of September at the ninth hour, just thirty-five days before his seventy-sixth birthday. His body was carried by the senators of the municipalities and colonies from Nola in southern Italy all the way to Bovillae, in the night time because of the season of the year, being placed by day in the basilica of the town at which they arrived or in its principal temple. At Bovillae the members of the equestrian order met it and bore it to Rome, where they placed it in the vestibule of his house.... There was even an official who took oath that he had seen the form of the Emperor, after he had been reduced to ashes, on its way to heaven.

54

CASSIUS DIO

Another Account of Augustus' Death
Third Century CE

In his account of Augustus' death, Cassius Dio provides his most explicit suggestion that Livia was responsible for it. Although Dio alludes to Octavian's atrocities during the civil wars, he confirms that as "princeps," Augustus was both humane and effective.

So Augustus fell sick and died. Livia incurred some suspicion in connection with his death, in view of the fact that he had secretly sailed over to the island to see Agrippa and seemed about to become completely reconciled with him. For she was afraid, some say, that Augustus would bring him back to make him sovereign, and so smeared with poison some figs that were still on trees from which Augustus

Cassius Dio, *Roman History* 56, 30; 43–45. Translated by Earnest Cary, Loeb Classical Library (Cambridge, Mass.: Harvard University Press, 1924).

was wont to gather the fruit with his own hands; then she ate those that had not been smeared, offering the poisoned ones to him. At any rate, from this or some other cause he became ill, and sending for his associates, he told them all his wishes, adding finally: "I found Rome of clay; I leave it to you of marble." He did not thereby refer literally to the appearance of its buildings, but rather to the strength of the Empire. And by asking them for their applause, after the manner of the comic actors, as if at the close of a mime, he ridiculed most tellingly the whole life of man.

Thus on the nineteenth day of August, the day on which he had first become consul, he passed away, having lived seventy-five years, ten months, and twenty-six days (he had been born on the twenty-third of September), and having been sole ruler, from the time of his victory at Actium forty-four years lacking thirteen days.

Not alone for these reasons did the Romans greatly miss him, but also because by combining monarchy with democracy he preserved their freedom for them and at the same time established order and security, so that they were free alike from the license of a democracy and from the insolence of a tyranny, living at once in a liberty of moderation and in a monarchy without terrors; they were subjects of royalty, yet not slaves, and citizens of a democracy, yet without discord.

If any of them remembered his former deeds in the course of the civil wars, they attributed them to the pressure of circumstances, and they thought it fair to seek for his real disposition in what he did after he was in undisputed possession of the supreme power; for this afforded in truth a mighty contrast. Anybody who examines his acts in detail can establish this fact; but summing them all up briefly, I may state that he put an end to all the factional discord, transferred the government in a way to give it the greatest power, and vastly strengthened it. Therefore, even if an occasional deed of violence did occur, as is apt to happen in extraordinary situations, one might more justly blame the circumstances themselves than him.

Now not the least factor in his glory was the length of his reign. For the majority as well as the more powerful of those who had lived under the Republic were now dead, and the later generation, knowing naught of that form of government and having been reared entirely or largely under existing conditions, were not only not displeased with them, familiar as they now were, but actually took delight in them, since they saw that their present state was better and more free from terror than that of which they knew by tradition.

Though the people understood all this during his lifetime, they nevertheless realized it more fully after he was gone; for human nature is so constituted that in good fortune it does not so fully perceive its happiness as it misses it when misfortune has come. This is what happened at that time in the case of Augustus. For when they found his successor Tiberius a different sort of man, they yearned for him who was gone. . . . At all events, the two emperors differed so completely from each other, that some suspected that Augustus, with full knowledge of Tiberius' character, had purposely appointed him his successor that his own glory might be enhanced thereby.

55

TACITUS

On the Funeral of Augustus
Second Century CE

Tacitus' account of the funeral includes imaginary arguments put forward to praise or condemn Augustus. Although it appears to be evenhanded, the author in fact devotes more time to the negative views of the emperor.

On the first day of the Senate Tiberius allowed nothing to be discussed but the funeral of Augustus, whose will, which was brought in by the Vestal virgins, named as his heirs Tiberius and Livia. The latter was to be admitted into the Julian family with the name of Augusta; next in expectation were the grand and great-grandchildren. In the third place, he had named the chief men of the State, most of whom he hated, simply out of ostentation and to win credit with posterity. His legacies were not beyond the scale of a private citizen, except a bequest of forty-three million five hundred thousand sesterces "to the

Tacitus, *Annals* 1, 8–10. Based on the translation of A. J. Church and W. J. Brodribb (London: Macmillan, 1886).

people and populace of Rome," of one thousand to every soldier in the praetorian guard, and of three hundred to every man in the legions composed of Roman citizens. . . .

On the day of the funeral soldiers stood round as a guard, amid much ridicule from those who had either themselves witnessed or who had heard from their parents of the famous day when slavery was still something fresh, and freedom had been resought in vain, when the slaying of Caesar, the Dictator, seemed to some the vilest, to others, the most glorious of deeds. "Now," they said, "an aged sovereign, whose power had lasted long, who had provided his heirs with abundant means to coerce the State, requires the defense of soldiers that his burial may be undisturbed."

Then followed much talk about Augustus himself, and many expressed an idle wonder that the same day marked the beginning of his assumption of empire and the close of his life, and, again, that he had ended his days at Nola in the same house and room as his father Octavius. People extolled too the number of his consulships, in which he had equaled Valerius Corvus and Gaius Marius combined,[1] the continuance for thirty-seven years of the tribunitian power, the title of Imperator twenty-one times earned,[2] and his other honors which had either frequently repeated or were wholly new. Sensible men, however, spoke variously of his life with praise and censure. Some said "that dutiful feeling toward a father, and the necessities of the State in which laws had then no place, drove him into civil war, which can neither be planned nor conducted on any right principles. He had often yielded to Antony, while he was taking vengeance on his father's murderers, often also to Lepidus. When the latter sank into feeble dotage and the former had been ruined by his profligacy, the only remedy for his distracted country was the rule of a single man. Yet the State had been organized under the name of neither a kingdom nor a dictatorship, but under that of a prince. The ocean and remote rivers were the boundaries of the Empire; the legions, provinces, fleets, all things were linked together; there was law for the citizens; there was respect shown to the allies. The capital had been embellished on a grand

---

[1] In the fourth century BCE, Valerius Corvus had held Rome's highest office, the consulship, six times, while Gaius Marius held it seven times between 106 and 86 BCE. Augustus' thirteen matched them both combined.

[2] During the Roman Republic successful generals were called *imperator* or "Commander" after great victories. Augustus was so acclaimed whenever his armies won a battle.

scale; only in a few instances had he resorted to force, simply to secure general tranquillity."

It was said, on the other hand, "that filial duty and State necessity were merely assumed as a mask. It was really from a lust for domination that he had excited the veterans by bribery, and had, when still a young man and a private citizen, raised an army, seduced away the consul's legions, and feigned an attachment to the faction of Pompey. Then, when by a decree of the Senate he had usurped the high functions and authority of praetor when Hirtius and Pansa were slain — whether they were destroyed by the enemy, or Pansa by poison infused into a wound, Hirtius by his own soldiers and Caesar's treacherous machinations — he at once took over both their armies, wrested the consulate from a reluctant Senate, and turned against the State the arms with which he had been entrusted against Antony. Citizens were proscribed, lands divided, without so much as the approval of those who executed these deeds. Even granting that the deaths of Cassius and of the Bruti were sacrifices to a hereditary enmity (though duty requires us to waive private feuds for the sake of the public welfare), still Pompey had been deluded by the phantom of peace, and Lepidus by the mask of friendship. Subsequently, Antony had been lured on by the treaties of Tarentum and Brundisium, and by his marriage with the sister, and paid by his death the penalty of a treacherous alliance. No doubt, there was peace after all this, but it was a peace stained with blood; there were the disasters of Lollius and Varus, the murders at Rome of the Varros, Egnatii, and Juli."[3]

The domestic life too of Augustus was not spared. "Nero's wife had been taken from him, and there had been the farce of consulting the pontiffs, whether, with a child conceived and not yet born, she could properly marry. There were the excesses of Quintus Tedius and Vedius Pollio; last of all, there was Livia, terrible to the State as a mother, terrible to the house of the Caesars as a stepmother. No honor was left for the gods, when Augustus chose to be himself worshipped with temples and statues, like those of the deities, and with priests in his name. He had not even adopted Tiberius as his successor out of affection or any regard to the State, but, having thoroughly seen his arrogant and savage temper, he had sought glory for himself

---

[3] Under Marcus Lollius in Gaul and Quinctilius Varus in Germany, Rome's armies suffered serious defeats, while in the capital Augustus had executed several political opponents and conspirators.

by a contrast of extreme wickedness." For, in fact, Augustus, a few years before, when he was a second time asking from the Senate the tribunician power for Tiberius, though his speech was complimentary, had thrown out certain hints as to his manners, style, and habits of life, which he meant as reproaches, while he seemed to excuse. However, when his obsequies had been duly performed, a temple with a religious ritual was decreed him.

56

SENECA

On the Clemency of Augustus
55 CE

The philosopher Seneca was the tutor of young Nero, and he continued to write speeches and provide counsel after the eighteen-year-old became emperor. In this section of his essay "On Clemency," Seneca urges Nero to look to his great-great-grandfather as a model for clemency.

By an example from your own family I wish to remind you how true this is. The deified Augustus was a mild prince if one should undertake to judge him from the time of his principate; but when he shared the state with others, he wielded the sword. When he was at your present age, having just passed his eighteenth year, he had already buried his dagger in the bosom of friends; he had already in stealth aimed a blow at the side of the consul, Mark Antony; he had already been a partner in proscription.

But when he had passed his fortieth year and was staying in Gaul, the information was brought to him that Lucius Cinna, a dull-witted man, was concocting a plot against him. He was told where and when and how he meant to attack him: one of the accomplices gave the information. . . .

Seneca, "On Clemency" 1, 9–11. In *Moral Essays,* translated by J. W. Basore, Loeb Classical Library (Cambridge, Mass.: Harvard University Press, 1928).

Not to fill up a great part of my book in repeating all his words—for he is known to have talked more than two hours, lengthening out this ordeal with which alone he intended to be content—at last he said: "Cinna, a second time I grant you your life; the first time you were an open enemy, now, a plotter and a parricide. From this day let there be a beginning of friendship between us; let us put to the test which one of us acts in better faith—I in granting you your life, or you in owing it to me." Later he, unsolicited, bestowed upon him the consulship, chiding him because he did not boldly stand for the office. He found Cinna most friendly and loyal, and even was named the heir to Cinna's property. No one plotted against him further.

Your great-great-grandfather spared the vanquished; for if he had not spared them, whom would he have had to rule? Sallustius and a Cocceius and a Deillius and the whole inner circle of his court he recruited from the camp of his opponents; and now it was his own mercifulness that gave him a Domitius, a Messala, an Asinius, a Cicero, and all the flowers of the state. What a long time was granted even Lepidus to die! For many years he suffered him to retain the insignia of a ruler, and only after the other's death did he permit the office of chief pontiff to be transferred to himself; for he preferred to have it called an honor rather than a spoil. This mercifulness led him on to safety and security, this made him popular and beloved, although the necks of the Roman people had not yet been humbled when he laid hand upon them; and today this preserves for him a reputation which is scarcely within the power of rulers even while they live. A god we believe him to be, but not because we are bidden; that Augustus was a good prince, that he well deserved the name of father, this we confess for no other reason than because he did not avenge with cruelty even the personal insults which usually sting a prince more than wrongs, because when he was the victim of lampoons he smiled, because he seemed to suffer punishment when he was exacting it, because he was so far from killing the various men whom he had convicted of intriguing with his daughter that he banished them for their greater safety, and gave them their credentials. Not merely to grant deliverance, but to guarantee it, when you know that there will be many to take up your quarrel and do you the favor of shedding an enemy's blood—this is really to forgive.

Such was Augustus when he was old, or just upon the verge of old age. In youth he was hot-headed, flared up with anger, and did many things which he looked back upon with regret. To compare the mildness of the deified Augustus with yours no one will dare, even if the

years of youth shall be brought into competition with an old age that
was more than ripe. Granted that he was restrained and merciful—
yes, to be sure, but it was after Actium's waters had been stained with
Roman blood, after his own and an enemy's fleet had been wrecked
off Sicily, after the holocaust of Perugia and the proscriptions. I,
surely, do not call weariness of cruelty mercy.

57

VELLEIUS PATERCULUS

A Soldier's View of Augustus

29 CE

*Velleius served under Tiberius while Augustus was emperor. Thus he had
a perspective very different from that of the haughty, jealous senators of
the capital. This is a rare view of the Augustan era from the rank-and-
file soldier. His praise of Augustus, Tiberius, and the entire family was
sincere.*

As for Caesar's return to Italy and to Rome—the procession which
met him, the enthusiasm of his reception by men of all classes, ages,
and ranks, and the magnificence of his triumphs and of the spectacles
which he gave—all this it would be impossible adequately to describe
even within the compass of a formal history, to say nothing of a work
so circumscribed as this. There is nothing that man can desire from
the gods, nothing that the gods can grant to a man, nothing that wish
can conceive or good fortune bring to pass, which Augustus on his
return to the city did not bestow upon the Republic, the Roman
people, and the world. The civil wars were ended after twenty years,
foreign wars suppressed, peace restored, the frenzy of arms everywhere lulled to rest; validity was restored to the laws, authority to the

Velleius Paterculus, *Compendium of Roman History* 1, 89. Translated by Frederick Ship-
ley, Loeb Classical Library (Cambridge, Mass.: Harvard University Press, 1924).

courts, and dignity to the Senate; the power of the magistrates was reduced to its former limits, with the sole exception that two were added to the eight existing praetors. The old traditional form of the Republic was restored. Agriculture returned to the fields, respect to religion, to mankind freedom from anxiety, and to each citizen his property rights were now assured; old laws were usefully emended, and new laws passed for the general good; the revision of the Senate, while not too drastic, was not lacking in severity. The chief men of the state who had won triumphs and had held high office were at the invitation of Augustus induced to adorn the city.

In the case of the consulship only, Caesar was not able to have his way, but was obliged to hold that office consecutively until the eleventh time in spite of his frequent efforts to prevent it; but the dictatorship which the people persistently offered him, he as stubbornly refused. To tell of the wars waged under his command, of the pacification of the world by his victories, of his many works at home and outside of Italy would weary a writer intending to devote his whole life to this one task. As for myself, remembering the proposed scope of my work, I have confined myself to setting before the eyes and minds of my readers a general picture of his principate.

58

PLINY THE ELDER

On the Trials and Tribulations of an Emperor
75 CE

In his sprawling encyclopedia, Natural History, *Pliny the Elder includes a vignette on the unhappiness of Augustus' life: his diseases, his disappointments, and the repeated heartbreak of his family life. It is an interesting counterpoint to the usual view that political power brings success and happiness. His book supports the idea that Julia's offense was not merely adultery but participation in a political conspiracy.*

Pliny the Elder, *Natural History* 7, 147–50. Based on the translation of H. Rackham, Loeb Classical Library (Cambridge, Mass.: Harvard University Press, 1942).

Also in the case of his late Majesty Augustus, whom the whole of
mankind enrolls in the list of happy men, if all the facts were carefully
weighed, great revolutions of man's lot could be discovered: his failure
with his uncle in regard to the office of Master of the Horse, when the
candidate opposing him, Lepidus, was preferred; the hatred caused by
the proscription; his association in the triumvirate with the wickedest
citizens, and that not with an equal share of power but with Antony
predominant; his flight in the battle of Philippi when he was suffering
from disease, and his three days' hiding in a marsh, in spite of his illness and his swollen dropsical condition (as stated by Agrippa and
Maecenas); his shipwreck off Sicily, and there also another period of
hiding in a cave; his entreaties to Proculeius to kill him, in the naval
rout when a detachment of the enemy was already pressing close at
hand; the anxiety of the struggle at Perugia, the alarm of the battle of
Actium, his fall from a tower in the Pannonian Wars; and all the
mutinies in his troops, all his critical illnesses, his suspicion of Marcellus' ambitions, the disgrace of Agrippa's banishment, the many plots
against his life, the charge of causing the death of his children; and
his sorrows that were not due solely to bereavement, his daughter's
adultery and the disclosure of her plots against her father's life, the
insolent withdrawal of his stepson Tiberius, another adultery, that of
his granddaughter; then the long series of misfortunes—lack of army
funds, rebellion of Illyria, enlistment of slaves, shortage of manpower,
plague at Rome and an occasional famine in Italy, resolve on suicide
and death more than half achieved by four days' starvation; next the
disaster of Varus and the foul slur upon his dignity; the disowning of
Agrippa Postumus after his adoption as heir, and the sense of loss that
followed his banishment; then his suspicion in regard to Fabius and
the betrayal of secrets; afterwards the intrigues of his wife and
Tiberius that tormented his latest days. In conclusion, this god—
whether deified more by his own action or by his merits I know not—
departed from life leaving his enemy's son his heir.

59

PHILO OF ALEXANDRIA

Jewish Praise for Augustus

39 CE

In 39 CE, the Jewish philosopher Philo of Alexandria went with a delegation to discourage the emperor Caligula from erecting his statue in the Temple of Jerusalem. In his appeal to the emperor, Philo included a panegyric to the emperor's great-grandfather, founder of the dynasty.

Again, why did you not pay similar honor to him who exceeded the common race of human nature in every virtue, who, by reason of the greatness of his absolute power and his own excellence, was the first man to be called Augustus, not receiving the title after another by a succession of blood as a part of his inheritance, but who was himself the origin of his successors, having that title and honor? He who first became emperor, when all the affairs of the state were in disorder and confusion; for the islands were in a state of war against the continents, and the continents were contending with the islands for the preeminence in honor, each having for their leaders and champions the most powerful and eminent of the Romans who were in office. And then again, great sections of Asia were contending against Europe, and Europe against Asia, for the chief power and dominion; the European and Asiatic nations rising up from the extremities of the earth, and waging terrible wars against one another over all the earth, and over every sea, with enormous armaments, so that very nearly the whole race of mankind would have been destroyed by mutual slaughter and made utterly to disappear, if it had not been for one man and leader, Augustus, by whose means they were brought to a better state, and therefore we may justly call him the averter of evil.

This is Caesar, who calmed the storms which were raging in every direction, who healed the common diseases which were afflicting both Greeks and barbarians, who descended from the south and from the

---

Philo, *Legation to Gaius* 143–49. Translated by Charles Yonge (London: G. Bell and Sons, 1854).

east, and ran on and penetrated as far as the north and the west, in such a way as to fill all the neighboring districts and waters with unexpected miseries.

This is he who did not only loosen but utterly abolish the bonds in which the whole of the habitable world was previously bound and weighed down. This is he who destroyed both the evident and the unseen wars which arose from the attacks of robbers. This is he who rendered the sea free from the vessels of pirates, and filled it with merchantmen.

This is he who gave freedom to every city, who brought disorder into order; who civilized and made obedient and harmonious, nations which before his time were unsociable, hostile, and brutal. This is he who increased Greece by many Greeces, and who Graecized the regions of the barbarians in their most important divisions: the guardian of peace, the distributor to every man of what was suited to him, the man who proffered to all the citizens favors with the most ungrudging liberality, who never once in his whole life concealed or reserved for himself any thing that was good or excellent.

Now this man who was so great a benefactor to them for the space of three and forty years, during which he reigned over Egypt, they passed over in silence and neglect, never erecting any thing in their synagogues to do him honor; no image, no statue, no inscription.

And yet if ever there was a man to whom it was proper that new and unprecedented honors should be voted, it was certainly fitting that such should be decreed to him, not only because he was as it were the origin and fountain of the family of Augustus, not because he was the first, and greatest, and universal benefactor, having, instead of the multitude of governors who existed before, entrusted the common vessel of the state to himself as one pilot of admirable skill in the science of government to steer and govern; for the verse,

The government of many is not good,

is very properly expressed, since a multitude of votes is the cause of every variety of evil; but also because the whole of the rest of the habitable world had decreed him honors equal to those of the Olympian gods.

A Glossary of Greek and Latin Terms

Capitoline Hill The Capitoline Hill (or Capitol) contained the temple of Jupiter Optimus Maximus ("Jupiter Best and Greatest").

censor Magistrate who conducted a "census" every five years, which listed all citizens, including their possessions, as well as senators.

centurion Officer in charge of a *century* of one hundred Roman legionaries.

circus Oval stadium used for chariot racing during the public games.

cohort An army unit of five hundred men, or a unit of the palace (praetorian) guard.

consul One of two highest officials of the Roman republic, elected annually to rule at Rome or command the army. During the Empire, their powers were greatly reduced. Consuls could be extended in power as **proconsuls** to govern provinces.

denarius (pl. **denarii**) Roman silver coin worth four sesterces.

dictator Single magistrate appointed with full powers when the state was seriously threatened but only for a limited term of six months or less. Changed by Julius Caesar into a permanent dictatorship.

eques, equites Originally members of the elite cavalry, but transformed by Augustus into a "class" just below the senators. The equestrians were a central element in the imperial civil service.

flamen Dialis Priest of Jupiter.

genius Protective spirit or deity of a family (*gens*); under the Empire, the worship of the emperor's *genius* was an aspect of the ruler cult.

imperator A title given to commanders by acclamation of their soldiers. Under the Empire, only given to members of the imperial family when a triumph was declared.

imperium Highest civil and military power, once held by dictators, consuls, and praetors. Under the Empire, it was reserved to the emperor, who could delegate it.

173

Italians Inhabitants of Italy who had become Roman citizens only after 88 BCE, but who were still excluded from high office and influence in the late Republic.

lares Family gods worshipped at household shrines; an altar of the *Lares Augusti* of the imperial family stood in each of the 265 districts of Rome.

legate A deputy of the emperor who served as governor of an imperial province; also the commander of a legion.

legion The basic unit of the Roman citizen-army; at full strength a legion had six thousand men.

patricians The Roman elite during the Republic; "patrician" was given as an honorific title by the emperors.

plebeians (or **plebs**) The common people of Rome.

pontifex maximus High priest of the Roman state.

populares Republican politicians who claimed to work on behalf of the people (*populus*).

praetor Roman magistrate who ranked below the **consul**. A **praetor** served for one year, but he was usually recalled as a **propraetor** to command an army or govern a province.

prefect of Egypt Equestrian who served as governor of Egypt and reported directly to Augustus.

prefect of the grain supply Equestrian official charged with the importation and distribution of grain.

prefect of the praetorian guard Equestrian commander of the palace guard.

prefect of the watch Equestrian official in command of the police and fire brigade.

princeps "First citizen"—title of the emperor. *Princeps senatus* had earlier been applied to the leading member of the Senate.

proconsul Former consul who served as governor of a province.

propraetor See **praetor**.

quaestor Annual magistracy concerned with financial administration.

Senate The Roman deliberative body to which all high officials belonged. A senator remained a member for life, or until he was expelled.

sestercius, sesterces Bronze coin that was the standard unit of Roman money; four sesterces equal one silver denarius. A denarius was regarded as a reasonable day's pay.

tribunician power During the Republic, the tribunes were regarded as defenders of the people. Augustus took over the power, giving him a range of powers, including the *veto*.

trireme   A ship with three banks of oars; a *bireme* had two banks.

triumph   A celebration staged by a successful military commander. In the Empire, triumphs were restricted to members of the imperial family.

triumvirate   Λ group of three men (*triumvirs*) who controlled the Roman state.

Vestal virgins   Six priestesses who maintained the sacred flame of the goddess Vesta and served as the custodians of wills.

A Chronology of Events Relating to Caesar Augustus and the Roman Empire (63 BCE–1453 CE)

63 BCE   Birth of Gaius Octavius (later Augustus)

60   Formation of First Triumvirate by Pompey, Crassus, and Julius Caesar

58–49   Julius Caesar serves as governor of Gaul

48   Caesar defeats Pompey at Pharsalus; Caesar meets Cleopatra

46   Octavian rides with Julius Caesar in his triumph

44   *March 15:* Assassination of Julius Caesar; Octavian takes inheritance and become Gaius Julius Caesar Octavianus

43   *April:* Both consuls killed at battle of Mutina; Octavian named consul

   November: Octavian, Marc Antony, and Lepidus form the Second Triumvirate

   December: Cicero murdered during the proscriptions

42   Battle of Philippi—Brutus and Cassius die

41   Antony meets Cleopatra at Tarsus and spends the winter in Alexandria

40   Revolt suppressed by Octavian at Perugia; Treaty of Brundisium; Antony marries Octavia; Octavian marries Scribonia

39   Treaty of Misenum between Octavian, Antony, and Sextus Pompey; Octavian divorces Scribonia, who later gives birth to his only child, Julia

38   Octavian marries Livia Drusilla

37 BCE	Renewal of the triumvirate
36	Sextus Pompey defeated; Lepidus under house arrest until his death in 12 BCE
	Antony's disastrous military campaign against Parthia
35–33	Octavian campaigns in Illyria
34	Antony defeats Armenia; celebrations and donations in Alexandria
32	End of the triumvirate
31	*September 2:* Antony defeated at the battle of Actium
30	Battle of Alexandria; Antony and Cleopatra die; Octavian becomes Pharaoh
29	Octavian celebrates triple triumph at Rome: Egypt, Greece, Illyricum
28	Octavian builds family mausoleum
	Octavian revises membership of the Senate, as he does again in 18 and 11 BCE
27	*January 13:* Republic restored to Senate and people; Octavian given *imperium*
	Octavian given the name of *Augustus*
27 BCE– 476 CE	Roman Empire
27– 25 BCE	Augustus in Gaul and Spain
25	Augustus' daughter, Julia, marries his nephew Claudius Marcellus
23	Serious illness of Augustus, who resigns consulship for tribunician power
	Marcellus dies
22–19	Augustus in Greece and Asia
22	Conspiracies and executions in Rome
21	Agrippa marries Julia, who gives birth to Gaius (20 BCE) and Lucius (17 BCE) Caesar
20	Peace with Parthia; Roman legionary standards surrendered to Tiberius
19	Virgil dies, returning from Greece in Augustus' entourage
18	Julian Laws on marriage; revised in 9 CE
17	Celebration of Secular Games; Augustus adopts grandsons Gaius and Lucius

16–	
13 BCE	Augustus in Gaul
13	Vote to build *Ara Pacis Augustae*
12	At death of Lepidus, Augustus elected *pontifex maximus;* Agrippa dies
	Temple of Roma and Augustus at Lugdunum dedicated
11	Tiberius marries Julia
9	*Ara Pacis Augustae* dedicated
8	Sixth month (*Sextilius*) is renamed *Augustus;* Horace dies
6	Tiberius goes into exile on the Greek island of Rhodes
4	Birth of Jesus Christ in Bethlehem; King Herod of Judaea dies
2	Augustus becomes *pater patriae;* Forum of Augustus dedicated; Julia exiled
2 CE	Lucius Caesar dies; Tiberius returns to Rome
4	Gaius Caesar dies; Augustus adopts Tiberius, who is given *imperium*
6–9	Tiberius puts down a rebellion in Pannonia on the Danube
9	Arminius destroys Varus' three legions in Germany
13	Augustus prepares his *Res Gestae*
14	Augustus dies; Tiberius acclaimed as emperor
29	Livia dies
68	Nero dies; Julio-Claudian dynasty ends
476	Last emperor in Rome: Romulus Augustulus
1453	Fall of the Roman (Byzantine) Empire in Constantinople to the Turks

Questions for Consideration

1. What major problems did the Roman republic face in the first century BCE? Could those problems have been solved by the senatorial leadership? Why or why not?

2. Some regard Augustus as a reformer, others as a revolutionary. In what ways did Augustus reform the Roman political system and allow it to continue, and in what ways did he construct a completely new political system?

3. What were Augustus' motivations in his continued attacks on Antony and Cleopatra in 31 and again in 30 BCE?

4. Why and how did Augustus continue to change the legal basis of his power during the 20s BCE?

5. In what ways are the ancient sources sympathetic or hostile to the women of the imperial family? Why? What do you think about Livia, based on the sources?

6. How did Augustus attempt to provide for succession to the throne?

7. Why did Augustus attempt such social reforms as his laws on marriage and the manumission of slaves?

8. How did Augustus use senators, equestrians, freedmen, and local officials to administer his vast Empire?

9. What were Augustus' policies toward the Jews?

10. The reign of Augustus Caesar is usually seen as the beginning of a glorious age. However, the historian Tacitus was very critical of Augustus and his political changes. What did Tacitus really want? What most bothered him about Augustus? Can we trust his account? Why or why not?

11. Examine the way Augustus used his family to secure power and ensure a peaceful succession. Which of his actions were traditional and which were unprecedented at Rome?

12. How successful were Augustus' policies toward the army?

13. How did the Roman poets of the Golden Age regard Augustus, and why?

14. How does the statue of the Prima Porta Augustus (see image on front cover) convey leadership and military prowess? What devices are used in the statue to portray this image? How otherwise did Augustus use art and architecture to reinforce his position and image at Rome?

15. Discuss later opinions on the achievements of Augustus. With whom do you agree, and why?

16. Octavian was portrayed as a bloodthirsty young man, while the later Augustus is the kindly "Father of the Country." Did Augustus really change, or is it just propaganda on both sides? Explain.

17. In what ways was Augustus' reunification of the Empire important for later European civilization?

18. If you were to write a historical novel about Augustus, what would be his chief characteristics? Who would play Augustus when you sell your novel to Hollywood?

Selected Bibliography

GENERAL BOOKS

The Cambridge Ancient History, vol. X, *The Augustan Empire, 43 BC–AD 69.* 2nd ed. Edited by A. K. Bowman, E. Champlin, and A. Lintott. Cambridge: Cambridge University Press, 1996.
Excellent chapters on the triumviral period (C. Pelling), Augustan politics (J. Crook), and the expansion of empire (E. Gruen) bring recent scholarship to bear on the period. Other important topical chapters treat the imperial court (A. Wallace-Hadrill), finances (D. Rathbone), the Senate and equestrians (R. Talbert), administration (A. Bowman), and the military (L. Keppie). Individual chapters are included on each province as well as such thematic issues as law (B. Frier), religion (S. Price), and social status (S. Treggiari).

Brunt, P. *Social Conflicts in the Roman Republic.* New York: Norton, 1971.
An excellent brief survey of the social conflicts that destabilized the Roman republic.

Campbell, J. B. *The Emperor and the Roman Army, 31 BC–AD 235.* Oxford: Clarendon Press, 1984.
Campbell organizes his material thematically rather than chronologically, but it provides an excellent perspective on how Augustus' military innovations continued and developed under his successors.

Carter, J. M. *The Battle of Actium: The Rise and Triumph of Augustus Caesar.* London: Hamilton, 1970.
A study of the background and the military and naval tactics used at Actium.

Crook, J. "Augustus: Power, Authority, Achievement." In *Cambridge Ancient History,* vol. X, 113–46.
An essay on how Augustus was able to establish his authority and an evaluation of his contributions to Roman history.

Earl, D. C. *The Age of Augustus.* London: Elek, 1970.
Although published as a lavishly illustrated coffee-table book, Earl's general essays are excellent.

Eck, W. *The Age of Augustus.* Oxford: Blackwell Publishing, 2003.
A recent, short description of the life of Augustus, with a new translation of the *Res Gestae.*

Hopkins, K. "Conquerers and Slaves: The Impact of Conquering an Empire on the Political Economy of Italy." In *Conquerers and Slaves: Sociological Studies in Roman History*. Cambridge: Cambridge University Press, 1978, 1–98.
Hopkins provides an overview of the effect of imperialism on the Roman domestic economy and Roman political life.

Millar, F., and E. Segal, eds. *Caesar Augustus: Seven Aspects*. Oxford: Clarendon Press, 1984.
Collected papers from a conference to honor Sir Ronald Syme's eightieth birthday.

Raaflaub, K., and M. Toher. *Between Republic and Empire: Interpretations of Augustus and His Principate*. Berkeley: University of California Press, 1990.
Papers collected to celebrate the fiftieth anniversary of the publication of Syme's *The Roman Revolution*. Among the nineteen papers are several by H. Galsterer, Z. Yavetz, and J. Linderski, which discuss Syme's contribution to our understanding of Augustus.

Southern, P. *Augustus*. New York: Routledge, 1998.
This is now the standard biography of Augustus in English.

Syme, R. *The Roman Revolution*. Oxford: Clarendon Press, 1939.
Syme's interpretation of Octavian's rise to power is in many ways dated; for example, he had little to say about art, religion, or the masses. Yet the seminal impact makes it the most important book on Augustus in the twentieth century.

Talbert, R. *The Senate of Imperial Rome*. Princeton, N.J.: Princeton University Press, 1984.
This book remains the standard examination of all aspects of the Roman Senate under the emperors.

Yavetz, Z. *Plebs and Princeps*. Oxford: Clarendon Press, 1969.
This monograph fills an important gap in our knowledge of the Roman masses under Augustus.

ANCIENT SOURCES

Appian. *The Civil Wars*. Translated by J. Carter. New York: Penguin Books, 1996.

Braud, D. *Augustus to Nero: A Sourcebook on Roman History 31 BC–AD 68*. New York: Barnes and Noble, 1985.
Braud translates both literary texts as well as inscriptions and the legends on Roman coins.

Brunt, P. A., and J. M. Moore. *Res Gestae divi Augusti*. Oxford: Oxford University Press, 1967.
Brunt and Moore provide a translation and a detailed historical commentary on Augustus' autobiographical text.

Cassius Dio. *The Roman History: The Reign of Augustus*. Translated by I. Scott-Kilvert. New York: Penguin Books, 1987.

Chisholm, K., and J. Ferguson, eds. *Rome: The Augustan Age.* Oxford: Oxford University Press, 1981.
This large collection of sources includes literary texts as well as many inscriptions.
Horace. *The Complete Odes and Epodes.* Translated by W. G. Shepherd. New York: Penguin Books, 1983.
Plutarch. *The Fall of the Roman Republic.* Rev. ed. Translated by R. Warner. New York: Penguin Books, 1972.
Includes lives of Cicero and Caesar.
Plutarch. *Makers of Rome.* Translated by I. Scott-Kilvert. New York: Penguin Books, 1965.
Includes lives of Brutus and Marc Antony.
Suetonius. *The Twelve Caesars.* Rev. ed. Translated by R. Graves. New York: Penguin Books, 1979.
Tacitus. *The Annals of Imperial Rome.* Rev. ed. Translated by M. Grant. New York: Penguin Books, 1996.
Virgil. *The Aeneid.* Translated by D. West. New York: Penguin Books, 1990.

AUGUSTAN CULTURE

Kenney, E. J., ed. *The Cambridge History of Classical Literature,* vol. 2. New York: Cambridge University Press, 1982.
Favro, D. *The Urban Image of Augustan Rome.* New York: Cambridge University Press, 1996.
Galinsky, K. *Augustan Culture: An Interpretative Introduction.* Princeton, N.J.: Princeton University Press, 1996.
Gurval, R. *Actium and Augustus: The Politics and Emotions of Civil War.* Ann Arbor. University of Michigan Press, 1995.
White, P. *Promised Verse: Poets in the Society of Augustan Rome.* Cambridge: Cambridge University Press, 1993.
Zanker, P. *The Power of Images in the Age of Augustus.* Translated by A. Shapiro. Ann Arbor: University of Michigan Press, 1988.

Acknowledgments

27. "An Outstanding Example of Pietas" from *As the Romans Did: A Source Book in Roman Social History,* Second Edition by Jo-Ann R. Shelton, translated by Jo-Ann R. Shelton, copyright © 1988, 1998 by Oxford University Press, Inc. Used by permission of Oxford University Press, Inc.

35. From *Ancient Roman Statutes: A Translation with Introduction, Commentary, Glossary, and Index* by Allan Chester Johnson, Paul Robinson Coleman-Norton, and Frank Card Bourne. Copyright © 1961. Courtesy of the University of Texas Press.

48. "Virgil, *A Description of the Battle of Actium,* 19 BCE." From *Aeneid* by Virgil, translated by David West (Penguin Books, 1990). Introduction and translation copyright © David West, 1990.

Index